Curmudgeon
How to Succeed as an Industry Analyst

Richard Stiennon

Cover image: Edward Binkley
Cover design: Karen Ethier
Interior design: Berenice Smith

Copyright 2020 by IT-Harvest Press, All rights reserved.

This publication may not be reproduced in print or digital form without the express permission of the author. Excerpts, quotes, and images may be used if the book is referenced.

Limits of Liability/Disclaimer of Warranty. While the publisher and author have used their best efforts in preparing this book, they make no representations or warranties with respect to the accuracy or completeness of the contents of this book and specifically disclaim any implied warranties of merchantability or fitness to or for a particular purpose. Neither the publisher or author shall be liable for any loss of profit or any other commercial damages.

IT-Harvest Press, LLC, Birmingham, Michigan, USA
www.ith-press.com

Curmudgeon: How to Succeed as an Industry Analyst
ISBN 978-1-945254-08-6

1st Printing
Printed in the United States of America

Table of Contents

	Foreword	v
	Introduction	viii
12	Are You Analyst Material?	
21	The Industry Analysis Business	
26	Duncan Chapple on the Industry Analyst Industry	
35	How to Be a Curmudgeon	
38	How to Become an Analyst	
51	The Analyst Path	
60	How to Write and Publish a Book	
72	Starting Your Own Firm	
89	The Influence Funnel	
118	Moving On or Growing Up	

Curmudgeon: How to Succeed as an Industry Analyst

127	Analyst Contributions
174	Success
177	Appendix I Writing Resources
179	Appendix II Analyst Firms

FOREWORD

Aviram Jenik, CEO Beyond Security

Richard and I first met around 2003. I was the young CEO of a security startup and Richard was the VP security research at Gartner—the highest ranking person in the most prestigious analyst organization in the security world, whose single hint of preference towards a vendor could translate immediately into millions of dollars in sales.

At that time, the Gartner "magic quadrant" was the definition of a self-fulfilling prophecy: its MQ 'leaders' would become the de-facto choice of almost any large enterprise while the vendors in the bottom left corner may just as well start packing, since no serious organization was going to buy an enterprise security product unless it comes with an endorsement from Gartner. Richard Stiennon was the person who placed vendors in the Quadrant—he was the emperor giving thumbs up or thumbs down to us vendors, the Gladiators in the Colosseum.

In methods that I prefer not to disclose right now I managed to get a 30 minute meeting with Richard during a brief visit to my city. I still vividly remember this meeting decades later. The one other person that was with us in the meeting room later described the meeting to me as "mutual love at first sight." It's an unusual way to describe a meeting between a vendor and an analyst, but that was an unusual meeting.

To explain how unconventional that meeting was to me, I need to give a bit of background about how vendor and analyst meetings usually go. Here's what should ordinarily happen: the vendor needs to impress the analyst while making sure not to offend anyone in the process (the downside of pissing off an analyst is immense, as I've learned later in my career). The analyst is there as both a source of infinite wisdom and also as a salesperson pitching a potential customer (Gartner makes money from vendors signing on to their consulting services).

So quite obviously, everyone is walking on eggshells throughout the meeting: the vendor gives compliments to everyone in the industry while subtly hinting that their solution is the best, and the analyst hems and haws non-committedly throughout the vendor presentation to later write a vague industry paper that is worded carefully to make sure everyone come out as heroes from this exercise. This is what I was expecting from my first meeting with the VP of security research for Gartner, and I couldn't have been more wrong.

Very early in my presentation I had a slide pointing out issues with IDS (Intrusion Detection Systems), at that time a multi-billion dollar industry with representation by virtually all the large security vendors. Knowing my place under the sun I tried to tone down my statements—already a difficult thing for a young, hot-blooded Israeli—but I couldn't help but notice to my surprise that Richard wasn't doing the expected hemming and hawing. Quite the opposite in fact—he was piling on the criticism. When I said IDS wasn't great, Richard interrupted and said it was utterly useless. Encouraged by this opening, I mentioned money spent on IDS is not an optimal investment and Richard corrected me to say "no, it's a complete waste of money." I then remember saying something like: "someone should be saying this publicly," to which Richard responded with: "I've already written it. It will go public very soon."

Things only got livelier from there: we agreed on a lot of things, loudly disagreed on a few others, and generally had a lot of fun. There was not an ounce of ambiguity in the entire hour of discussion (I was able to stretch my 30 minute slot) and I believe eventually Richard's Gartner handler had to pull me out of the room almost forcefully—I was just one of more than a dozen meetings Richard had that day, and definitely one of the least important ones. In any case, I figured that was the end of it. My company had no money to become a Gartner customer, and I knew no analyst can ever go public with a negative sentiment about a billion dollar IDS market. I also figured I would never talk to Richard again. I was wrong on all fronts.

It turns out that just a little later in that same year, Richard had made his opinion on Intrusion Detection Systems known, and it could not be more unambiguous. He called IDS "a market failure," basically telling most Gartner enterprise customers, the ones paying his salary, that they were fools for wasting millions on this useless technology. He continued by criticizing the supposed next generation technology (IPS) and the industry gave his analysis the title "IDS is Dead." It wasn't just a kid telling the emperor he has no clothes—it was the high-paid clothing consultant hired by the emperor telling him he's naked

Foreword

and doing it via an op-ed in the *New York Times*. It was the most direct kill shot ever made by an analyst to a vendor, and this one was aimed not at one, but at a group of the most powerful vendors in existence. The point was made: if you ask Richard a question, be prepared for him to give you an answer. Not that it matters, but he was right, of course. IDS became obsolete within the year and their supposed replacement, IPS, went the way of the dodo not long after.

Since that meeting and over the years, I tried to meet Richard every chance I had. To every such meeting I came armed with lots of questions and more often than not, his answers were my 'to-do' list in the weeks and months that followed. Some of these answers made it into his books: how to do analyst relations with a budget of zero dollars, how to get into the coveted upper right quadrant, who started the first nation-level cyber attack, and why did the hacker Adrian Lamo really surrender to the FBI. Other answers, like what vanity license plate to get as a company founder and how to get your ad in front of the CEO of the company you're selling to, I'll keep with me (why give up my competitive advantage?). None of these answers were ever vague, ambiguous, or boring. All of them were practical, refreshing, and thought provoking.

There's a reason why, 20 years later, Richard's "IDS is dead" analysis paper is still memorable. It was a once-in-a-generation event that is unlikely to be reproduced. In a perfect world, analysts would write their actual opinions, even if that opinion is "the million dollar product you bought, Mr. Customer, is already obsolete." They would answer questions and not try to validate the existing consensus opinion. I know what that world would look like because I had a chance to see a glimpse of it.

Anyone who knows Richard will attest that he is smart. But being in the technology field means being surrounded by smart people, to the point where it's almost a commodity. Being smart and practical, however, is much more valuable and much rarer. A typical smart analyst would ask him or herself: "how can I make sure my analysis is correct?" and reach the wrong conclusion: you can always be correct if your analysis is toned-down and vague enough. This is why so many analyst papers resemble astrology. Being practical means, as Richard explains in these pages, that to be "mostly right," you need to be "sometimes wrong" (or more accurately "about 20% wrong," because metrics are important), which leads to the Richard Stiennon litmus test for judging the quality of an analyst: "Do vendors lobby to have the analyst fired?"

Now, if you want Richard to teach you how to be an analyst, these next pages will do just that. Just keep in mind that before you go ahead and ask the question, buckle up and make sure you are ready for the straight answer.

INTRODUCTION

In 2012 I published what was intended to be the second of a pair of books about industry analysts, *UP and to the RIGHT, Strategy and Tactics of Analyst Influence*. I had already started *Curmudgeon*, but I happened to meet with Gene Kim, who had recently sold his company Tripwire to Belden. Gene was reaching out to the many people he had worked with in the industry over the years with a simple question: "How can I help you?" I gladly agreed to meet him on the outskirts of Ann Arbor. We talked for over three hours while Gene took notes of things to follow up on. He was making plans to write and publish his own book on DevOps, *The Phoenix Project*, so we had a great time talking about book publishing. I was exploring the self-publishing route for my next book, intended to be *Curmudgeon*. I described how there were going to be two books on the analyst business, one from the perspective of an analyst, and one for the vendors who wished to influence the analysts.

Rarely does a single conversation change one's plans. When I told Gene I often consulted with vendors on how to influence Gartner to improve a company's position on the infamous Magic Quadrant, Gene said, "If I had known you were doing that, we would have paid you more than we paid Gartner!" That is all it took to put *Curmudgeon* on the back burner and begin work on *UP and to the RIGHT*.

I wrote *UP and to the RIGHT* in a burst of writing frenzy. The bulk of the rough draft was written in a week at retreat in Tennessee. Within a month it was available as paperback and ebook on Amazon. Of everything I have written, *UP and to the RIGHT* has received the most positive response. Gartner analysts blogged about it and several had told me they recommend it to all of their vendor clients. Gartner salespeople purchase copies and send them on to their prospects and clients.

I calculated that there must be 20,000 analyst relations and PR professionals that would need my book. A little over 10% of them have purchased it. Not great

Introduction

numbers for the only book ever written on a topic, but not to worry. Gene's comment about spending on the related coaching made the resultant financial outcome well worth the time sunk into writing the book.

But I am more interested in the analyst business than the analyst relations business, so it is time to bring out *Curmudgeon: How to Succeed as an Industry Analyst*.

About the title. First, do you really have to be a curmudgeon to succeed? And second, what is success?

No, of course you do not need to self-identify as a curmudgeon, to be an analyst. As a matter of fact the traits associated with curmudgeon are probably things you should strive to avoid. This word associated with being an analyst was introduced to me at Gartner boot camp in Stamford, Connecticut. Most of boot camp is devoted to learning the archaic formulas for Gartner research, the Research Note (RN) and the famous probabilities assigned to predictions: "The market for books on industry analyst relations is going to double in 2020 (.9)." The boot camp also covered how to use the client inquiry system based on Lotus Notes, and of course, the Gartner Magic Quadrant

The highlight of the four-day boot camp was a lecture from Ken McGee, one of the most senior analysts. The title of his talk: How to Be a Curmudgeon. Ken's advice was meant to convey that which sets a good analyst apart from say a market researcher, or even a tech journalist. One nugget he imparted: "You should be wrong at least 20% of the time." In other words, if you are always right in your prognostications you are probably not stretching enough, not looking far enough in the future, and certainly will not have an impact on the way people think or engage their minds.

It turns out that being a curmudgeon may even be good for your brain health. A recent study out of Geneva concluded that "people who are less agreeable but with a natural curiosity and little conformism show better preservation of the brain regions that tend to lose volume, both in normal aging and in Alzheimer's disease." Less agreeable, curious, non-conformism. These sound like the prerequisites for an industry analyst.

Thus we have the origins of the title. But what about the "success" part? What is success? Should we measure it by financial success? Most of the analysts I know appear to be comfortably retired now. Members of The Analyst Syndicate, a group of mostly retired Gartner analysts, join a weekly video conference from very nice homes in very nice locations. Several own boats. Just being retired is, to me, a sign of success. Before the financial crisis of 2008-9, Rob Enderle, the analyst most known for covering Microsoft for the past two decades, was blogging about becoming an ex-pat in Turks and Caicos. Living in the Caribbean while continuing to work as an independent analyst certainly meets my aspirations of success.

So, making enough money to retire on is one measure of success. There are other measures. One is influence. At Gartner they measured influence by number of times an analyst was quoted in major media, which included the *LA Times*, *Washington Post*, *Wall Street Journal*, *USA Today*, the *New York Times*, and the wire services. In the four years I was at Gartner I was quoted in all of those outlets. There were analysts who were quoted ten times more that I was. They were always at the top of the rankings. Quotes are one measure, what about impact? How is that measured? Look beyond quotes and find responses from the industry. Did the vendors change their product direction, or at the very least, the language they use to describe their product strategy in response to something the analyst said or wrote? Do vendor representatives vehemently respond and write vitriolic blog posts about "ivory tower analysts?" Do vendors lobby to have the analyst fired? Or, in the famous case of Betsy Burton, who criticized a new version of Oracle DB, does a rich and powerful CEO (Larry Ellison) lash out by canceling analyst firm contracts in response?

Larry Ellison is quoted in *Softwar: An Intimate Portrait of Larry Ellison and Oracle*:

> Betsy Burton uses a more random approach: she publishes her results without any supporting data or details about her methodology. You can't check a damn thing. You have to take her word for it.

Burton's reputation was certainly enhanced by this episode. Sometimes picking fights with a bully can be a good thing.

You will ultimately have to judge what success is for yourself. I assure you, that the financial success possible from choosing a career as an analyst pales compared to being a founder of a startup that goes public. If you stay in the business a few years you will know many of those. You may even influence the trajectory of their products and companies. If you peg "success" at tens of millions in net worth, you are probably not going to achieve that as an analyst. But another definition of success, one that will be appreciated by writers, musicians, and artists, is "being afforded a living doing what you love." That is achievable and that is what this book may help you achieve.

There are many paths to becoming an industry analyst. I include my own story interwoven with what I have learned. I also reached out to other industry analysts to get their stories to provide multiple perspectives. I am grateful to them for their contributions: Tom Austin, recently retired from a 24-year career at Gartner and the founder of The Analyst Syndicate; Bob Hafner, who

Introduction

recruited and hired me into Gartner in the fall of 2000; Jon Oltsik, an Enterprise Strategy Group analyst; Greg Young, who took over for me at Gartner; and Mark Bouchard, an analyst who is so curmudgeonly he refused to join Gartner when META Group was acquired and struck off on his own. Anton Chuvakin, a prolific writer who left Gartner to join a large technology firm, provides his perspective too. Duncan Chapple of the Analyst Observatory also shares his thoughts garnered from decades of studying the analyst business.

Are You Analyst Material?

Do you really want to be an industry analyst? To answer that question, let's start with a little history. Gideon Gartner, arguably the inventor of the space, created the Gartner Group in 1997, one of the first industry analyst firms. The purpose of the firm was to give buy-hold-sell advice to its clients, but for technology, not stocks. An industry analyst is a subject matter expert that knows the industry, its products, its people, and its trends. Quite often the analyst drives those trends through influence, forecasts, and published research. Yes, an analyst provides product purchase advice, but there is much more to it. An industry analyst is an advocate for the industry, often giving it a voice, representing and explaining the industry to the wider world. This communication comes through research reports, keynote addresses, columns and blogs, and as a frequently quoted expert in major media.

An analyst is not a journalist, not a consultant, and not solely a public speaker. Yet, he or she must be able to write, provide advice, and speak in front of large groups. All of these capabilities and the traits given below make for a good analyst. Deciding if you want to be an analyst will depend on which of these activities you enjoy doing and which of these traits you think you have.

You have probably already encountered industry analysts in your own field. If you are in the technology space, you have read, heard, or even met analysts from Gartner, Forrester, IDC, Ovum, or any of the dozens of smaller firms. You may even be familiar with one of the hundreds of independent analysts such as Rob Enderle, Johna Till Johnson, Zeus Kerravala or, ahem, me. But seeing or hearing their output is not likely to give you a clear idea of what an analyst does. This book will give you a complete understanding of not only what an industry analyst does, but how to become one.

To help you decide whether you want to be an industry analyst, let's first address the downside. Then balance that against the upside, and you make the decision.

The Downside
Being an industry analyst, whether independent or employed by a firm, is a lot of work. There are deadlines for research and quotas (self-imposed if you are independent). As you grow in influence, demands on your time increase. There will be conferences to keynote, client inquiries to respond to, and vendor briefings to sit through; all while maintaining what many would consider an insane travel schedule. If you are at one of the big firms, you have to support their week-long conferences with presentations, client meetings, and social events.

What about the pay? It's good, but not great. A neophyte analyst, even with five to ten years industry experience, may make as little as $90k. Even the top rung analysts at the big firms rarely make more than $250k and that is after twenty years of experience.

The travel is grueling. Many analysts get on a plane at least fifty times a year. On that plane they catch up on their writing or reading. In the airports they field client calls and briefings from vendors. In their hotel rooms they take calls from overseas and from their management or fellow analysts

Analysts are typically individual contributors. They do not have research assistants to help collect, compile, and organize information. They do not have administrative assistants to coordinate travel, handle expenses, or schedule calls. What they do have is a plethora of people who make demands on their time: Management looking for participation in coordinating a conference; the client inquiry desk asking to open up more time slots for client calls; the consulting arm looking for support on their projects; the sales team wanting support on closing a new prospect; and, of course, clients. In the meantime the analyst is scheduling and paying for flights, hotel rooms, and rental cars and desperately trying to catch up on reporting those expenses, along with phone, internet, and health costs. Somehow the analyst has to find time to formulate, compose, and write research reports and create presentations. It is grueling work.

The Upside
If the downside has you thinking about slinking back to your cozy desk job with 20% travel and three weeks of vacation with generous stock options, take a moment to consider the upside. As an industry analyst you can have tremendous impact on your space. You can prevent your clients from making costly product selection mistakes. You can change the direction an industry takes as it grows and develops. You can act as a connector by introducing vendors to each other

when their technologies could benefit from working together. You can help vendors in their acquisition or spin-off plans. You can guide startups down the right path to success. You can help investors make the right decisions. And, if you are the type that appreciates recognition, you can build a reputation for your insights, advice, and guidance that pays immeasurable dividends in self-satisfaction.

Besides all that, being an analyst can be the ideal job for someone with the traits listed in the coming pages. It feeds your desire to learn everything about your industry. Every minute spent talking to end users, getting briefed by vendors, watching demo videos on YouTube, and reading about your industry, is time well spent and justified. There is perhaps nothing as satisfying as knowing your space better than anyone else and being completely confident in your assessments.

The money can be good, too. There is a cap on what you can earn at one of the big firms but many analysts get hired away from these firms to executive positions in industry. Their reputation as an influencer and expert commands high salaries, and joining a pre-IPO vendor can be very lucrative. And then there is the independent route, which can lead to a very comfortable living and expose you to even greater opportunities in the future. Think how quickly the money adds up if you can command speaking fees of $12,000 and charge $1,000/hr for your expert advice!

What is the difference between an analyst and a consultant?

Many of the traits listed in this chapter are shared between analysts and consultants. Often consultants are subject matter experts and they are usually great presenters and even good writers. But the business models and their contributions are completely different. The typical management consultant is a generalist who can quickly adapt a set of tools and processes to a new challenge, be it a restructuring, process improvement, or strategic engagement. Consultants have intense, often long term interactions with their clients. There is a lot of interviewing, compiling, and frankly regurgitating in the consulting business. Industry analysts on the other hand are acknowledged experts in their space. Their research into industry practices turns into their base of knowledge, which they share with clients on demand. A typical engagement for an analyst lasts a day, not weeks. The analyst listens to the client's presentations on their current practices and tools and the issues they have identified. The analyst then draws on his or her extensive knowledge of hundreds of similar organizations and spells out any deficiencies, or opportunities for improvement. The first encounter with an analyst can be refreshing or abruptly shocking. A consultant asks questions to help him or her get up to speed on your industry. The analyst asks questions that allow him or her to judge the maturity of your technology deployment. What is the makeup of your staff? What tools do you use? Have you investigated these other tools? The analyst will then simply tell you what you should do.

Many people have never had an opportunity to experience this type of interaction with an analyst. Their perception of analysts as pundits and pontificators is based on seeing the analyst present or reading their research reports. As a neophyte analyst at Gartner, I went along with a senior analyst on a day trip to a startup in the secure file transfer business. I had the technical background to participate as I had helped another such company with an end-to-end security review of their offering. This veteran analyst had worked with dozens of startups. His questions and hard hitting guidance struck me as well worth the huge fee Gartner charges for such strategic engagements. Now, after seventeen years as an industry analyst, I too have worked with hundreds of technology startups. I can see their future and the decisions they will have to make in the ensuing months as if their timelines were already charted before my eyes. I can immediately identify issues with their go-to-market message, their sales and channel strategy, and holes in their talent pool. As they present, I usually jot down a dozen opportunities for them to partner with other vendors, or candidates to sit on their boards and generate business opportunities, or resellers that would be interested in their products, or investors that have expressed an interest in their space. Of course, an analyst shares all of this information and holds nothing back. The engagement fee has already been paid and they are there to earn that fee.

A consultant would be aghast at the idea of giving away all these golden nuggets of wisdom at the first meeting! Instead, they would hold back, sketch out a plan of attack, and contract for as long term a project as possible.

Who makes a good analyst?

Before making your final decision, consider these traits of a good analyst. Not all analysts will have all of these traits, of course. But if you begin to recognize yourself here, you will probably make a great analyst.

Unquenchable thirst for knowledge

The one key to determining if someone is cut out to be a great industry analyst is her predilection to learn. Multiple degrees could be an indicator, but far more likely is that you spend your spare time reading and gaining knowledge. When you take on a new hobby or pastime, do you research it extensively? Take notes?

Keep a folder of articles on your computer? When you travel, do you research the area you are going to? Study its history? Visit museums and historical sites? Do you find yourself seeing an interesting article online and following it down the rabbit hole? Do you suddenly realize that you have just spent an hour on Wikipedia, Google Scholar, or YouTube, learning everything you can about some random topic? Does your productivity at work suffer because you are more interested in learning new things than going to meetings? You may well be analyst material.

Love your space
You love your space. You research everything about it: the people, technologies, companies, and products. You spend evenings and weekends reading books written by key people or articles that have had an impact on your field. You are constantly struck by insights and new ideas about your space. You know you have this trait when a clear vision of the future of your space hits you in the shower, causing an endorphin rush that is hard to match.

Analytical
Analysts love data. Show an analyst a bar graph and their eyes will get intense as they absorb the data, then they will glaze over as they ponder the implications, and finally they may light up with that "aha!" as they derive some insight. There will also be questions. How was the data collected? What is the error? What are the causes? What are the biases that could have skewed the data? What additional information is needed? How could the data be improved? If you really want to distract an analyst, expose him or her to an infographic!

Questions status quo
An analyst looks at what is and asks, what could change? Is this the best state? What is wrong with the current accepted practice? Is this industry reaching maturity and ready to be reinvented? Is the status quo able to address the macro changes represented by changing economies, demographics, or climate?

Questions everything
An analyst questions every assertion. Anything stated as fact has to be supported. Seeing the words "best," "most," "leading," or any superlative applied to a product, process, or solution will cause an analyst to stop and question. An analyst is a skeptic.

Stubborn
Once an analyst comes to a conclusion, it is extremely difficult to sway her away from her convictions. Objections may cause her to re-think her conclusions but invariably leads to stronger supporting arguments.

Honest
That said, once confronted with evidence that refutes her position, an analyst will immediately admit to being wrong and move on. Being an analyst does not mean always being right, as Ken McGee said. Tom Austin, who was one of the most senior analysts at Gartner, says: "Great analysts take risks. Not too crazy. They need to be right a little more often than wrong. Analysts who are always right aren't bold enough."

An analyst hates subterfuge and lying. His own honesty has tuned his senses to recognize dishonesty in others. He has no patience for marketing hype. He is apt to appear abrupt because he does not couch his advice in platitudes. It will be hard hitting, critical, and to the point.

Objective
This is a tricky trait to identify. Everyone likes to think they are objective. In an analyst, the trait is shown by the ability to separate personal desires or benefits from their analysis. Can you recognize when the team playing your home town favorite is better than yours? Can you admit that your favorite political candidate has faults? Can you see both sides in a conflict?

Thinks about the future
Analysts are fascinated by the future. They look for trends. They study the world and ask what identifiable changes will mean for the future. How does an aging populace affect the market? How does the cloud impact this business? Will wearable computing change health care? Will life extension change anything? Will the eradication of some disease change the path of developing nations? Will a global pandemic change the way we work and interact? Do cyber weapons have the potential to upset the balance of power?

Insatiable reader
Analysts read; newspapers, magazines, books, the back of the cereal box, anything they can get their hands on. They tend towards nonfiction and will read anything about their space. If they watch TV it is for documentaries and news.

Good at analogies
Good analysts are able to draw comparisons and create pithy analogies. Some, like me, have to work harder at coming up with good analogies than others, but this trait is a valuable one to have or develop.

Productive
Analysts are productive. They have the ability to churn out an amazing amount of content. It can be formal white papers, columns, or blog posts. They have so much to say they cannot stop from spewing advice.

Motivated
Successful analysts are motivated to stay on top of their space. They produce content on airplanes, in doctors' waiting rooms, even while on conference calls.

Showman
Analysts have no problem with being the center of attention. They make unequivocal statements. They are proud of their charts and plots, their pregnant pause, their punch line.

Not afraid of public speaking
I once went to a global meeting of PwC managers. Part of the entertainment on the first day was a dynamic motivational speaker. He cited the oft-repeated statistic that the most common phobia is the fear of public speaking. He asked the audience of 600 managers from one of the largest consulting firms in the world for a show of hands: who had a fear of speaking in public? Not a single person raised their hand. He accused us of lying! He did not realize that you do not become a manager at PwC unless you are completely comfortable getting up in front of a crowd and presenting. While many people do indeed have this fear, most consultants, and certainly industry analysts, don't. Many may have at one time, but the process of becoming a successful analyst involves lots of opportunities to speak in public. Over time, analysts get over that fear and even have to learn techniques to tap into that remembered fear to inject a little energy into their pitches.

Empathetic
A valuable trait for an analyst is the ability to discern the perspective of a client. They ask questions and delve into the particular problems a client is trying to solve. It could be a vendor who is frustrated with the failure of their market to

grow or an end user who is striving to overcome a technical or human resource issue. An analyst will empathize.

Storyteller
Analysts love telling stories. Have dinner with an analyst and you will be subjected to a constant stream of stories. Practically any topic raised will generate a new story from an analyst, often to a fault. They don't just make a point or state an opinion, they back it up with a corroborating story.

Opinionated
Analysts have opinions on everything. They take sides. They are not happy with the "wait and see" attitude. They are anxious to predict what will happen. They use every situation to test their predictive ability.

Ability to recognize patterns
Analysts look for patterns in everything. Two occurrences of the same question or situation make a pattern. Three are a possible trend. They compare what they know with what they learn to see if it fits.

Predictive
Analysts are not afraid to make predictions. A merger or acquisition in their industry gives rise to "what this means for end users," and "what this means for competitors." They derive great satisfaction out of being right while being wrong does not prevent them from making more predictions.

Wordsmith
Analysts love words. They are critical readers. They love a good metaphor. They study writing and communication skills. The meanings of words are important to them. Once, at Gartner, I was asked to submit a presentation for a big conference in Cannes. In my slide deck I used the phrase "Achilles heel" to describe a fault in a technology. I was told that "Achilles heel" was an American colloquialism and I was not allowed to use it in front of a European audience. My response was "Excuse me? The capital of France is named for the guy who shot Achilles in his heel!" It may have been a cliché, but was most certainly not a colloquialism.

Thick-skinned
This trait definitely did not describe me when I joined Gartner. I was overly concerned about what people thought about me and did not take verbal attacks

well. But, one of my most formative experiences was living through the outrage and criticism directed at me for declaring a particular technology not worth the time and expense of deploying. The vendors of that technology in particular attempted to completely discredit me. "Ivory tower analyst" was the softest epithet hurled my way.

Don't be disheartened if you do not have all of these traits. They are not required, just indicators that being an analyst might be right for you. If, on the other hand, you hate writing, don't really enjoy your field, and have trouble seeing patterns in things, you may want to consider another occupation.

What fields give rise to good analysts? Great question. Good analysts come from all walks of life. I have known engineers, journalists, consultants, concert venue bouncers, and even particle physicists who have become great analysts. The one aspect that you must have is you must be an expert in your field. I use Malcolm Gladwell's identifier of expertise: having devoted at least 10,000 waking hours to your field. That equates to five working years. By the time you gain that experience, you are probably at least 30 years old. You probably already write about your space, even if only a blog. You probably have given hundreds of presentations even if not many are keynotes at major conferences. I will address the task of becoming an *acknowledged* expert in a later chapter.

If you see yourself reflected in these traits, and the hard work does not turn you off, read on. This book will strive to give you what you need to know in order to succeed as an industry analyst.

The Industry Analysis Business

A brief history of the industry
In order to better understand the business you are in, or hope to get into, it helps to know its history. In terms of business history, the analyst business is still very young. It dates back to only 1964.

There have been industry analysts, of course, probably since there has been industry. But it was the rise of technology that gave birth to the first industry analyst firms: Gartner, IDC, Forrester, and the Yankee Group in the US. These firms borrowed heavily from the business model of Wall Street analysts. These *stock* analysts are experts in understanding the securities of publicly traded companies as well as the many derivatives that have sprung up over the years. They evolved the simplistic buy-hold-sell ratings of stocks and bonds to guide their investor clients. Specialists in each investment sector arose who had deep knowledge about the represented companies, their management, and even their products. They would research the companies and the markets they sold into in the hopes of being able to offer good advice.

It was Gideon Gartner who is credited with recognizing that the advent of computer mainframes created a new opportunity. Technology research analysts, subject matter experts in mainframes and the software that ran on them, could offer advice to the large companies making purchasing decisions. In Gideon's words, they "provided buy-hold-sell guidance for technology." I believe there are opportunities for industry analysts in every field, be it oil and gas production, cars and trucks, agricultural equipment, drones, 3D printing, or alternative energy. In technology there are new sectors every year with Cloud, Machine Learning, Artificial Intelligence, Virtual Reality, and Augmented Reality, all in the stages where an industry analyst could prosper by covering them. There is a need for subject matter experts who know the players, the history, what works and what doesn't in each of these areas. Technology in particular moves so fast that it generates and maintains the demand for industry analysts. At a recent

Curmudgeon: How to Succeed as an Industry Analyst

event put on by America's Growth Capital, I was stunned by the number of new vendors present. There were 80 vendors in cyber security that I had never heard of, and that is my space. I was struck with the question, "How could anybody sort through all of these companies?" Then it dawned on me. Of course, that is the role of industry analysts.

Gartner Group, Inc. was founded by Gideon Gartner in 1979. Gideon had spent several years at IBM where he worked on competitive intelligence. He had a mechanical engineering degree from MIT and an MS from Sloan School of Management. He had left IBM to work at Oppenheimer & Co. where he was a research analyst (for equities). So it is no wonder that he had the background to form an advisory company that could help client companies purchase main frame technology. He and David Stein launched the Gartner Group with $675k in backing. That would be $2.2 million in today's dollars. It might be a useful exercise to think about the fact that IBM's revenue at the time was $22 billion. If you are launching an analyst firm, make sure the space is big enough to create the demand for your service.

Gartner Group went through several early gyrations. First, it went public in 1985. Then, only three years later, it was acquired by Saatchi & Saatchi, the advertising agency, for $90.3 million. By 1990 Saatchi & Saatchi had to divest and Gartner Group went through a management buyout backed by Bain Capital and Dun & Bradstreet. Gideon took a back seat at this point and Manny Fernandez was appointed President and CEO. By 1993 Gideon sold all of his stock and was no longer part of the company he founded.

Business started to boom for Gartner Group in 1995 with $25.5 million in earnings from sales of $229.2 million. That same year it acquired Dataquest, its major competitor. Dataquest was a market research firm that collated numbers on sales of technology products. In 1995 Gartner's products were still in the form of written research notes that were mailed to subscribers, including the infamous Magic Quadrant reports. By the time I joined the Gartner Group in 2000 there were still vestiges of the print paradigm around. But Gartner Group changed its name to just Gartner, and moved into the digital era in the early 2000s.

There are lots of crazy stories about the early days of the Gartner Group told by old timers; regular Friday afternoon meetings that involved Oprah-like shenanigans like envelopes full of money taped under chairs, or some sort of money tornado that blew dollar bills into the air and the lucky analyst being recognized would get a chance to grab as much as she could. If you ever get a chance, buy a Gartner pioneering analyst a drink and ask him about those days.

In April 2020 Gartner had a market capitalization of $9.2 billion and 2019 revenue of $4.25 billion. Most of that money came from research, with the balance coming from consulting and events. Just prior to the onset of the market decline due to COVID-19 Gartner's market cap was $14.5 billion. Gartner continues to make strategic acquisitions with a $2.6 billion purchase of CEB in early 2017.

Note that Gartner claims 12,000 corporate clients; only a 20% growth in the 14 years since I was at Gartner. Most of Gartner's strategy is to sell and package more services to their existing client base. Vendors of IT products view Gartner as impactful because those 12,000 clients are the largest organizations in the world. It is well worth studying Gartner. As an independent analyst, you are going to compete with Gartner. It sets the high bar for pricing. A typical first-time vendor client pays Gartner $50-100k a year for access to research and $25k for a day of strategic engagement with an analyst.

IDC

Like Gideon Gartner, Patrick J. McGovern also attended MIT. He founded International Data Corporation (IDC) in 1964 to fulfill a research contract from competitors of IBM like Univac, Xerox, and Burroughs. Initially IDC, like Dataquest, was focused on the numbers. It was a true market research firm.

McGovern branched out quickly into publishing with *Computerworld* and events with the ComNet Trade Show. He formed International Data Group (IDG) as a holding company for all of his businesses in 1967. McGovern went on to lead a media empire and was on the inaugural Forbes 400 list of America's richest in 1982. When he passed away in March 2014 he was ranked 244 in the world in terms of net worth. McGovern was reputed to have a photographic memory and could rattle off numbers on stage to great effect.

IDC is a small component of the IDG empire, which includes 200 magazines, 460 websites, and 700 events in 79 countries around the world. Yet it claims to employ 1,100 research analysts worldwide. True to its roots, IDC analysts are focused more on numbers than product features and capabilities. One IDC product that I have experience with is a massive spreadsheet, updated every quarter, which lists the network security appliances of every vendor with unit sales and revenue broken down by region. Pivot tables allow a client to look at market segment, region, and price ranges for every product category. The methodology involves polling each vendor, and not surprisingly, the customers for the spreadsheet are most of the large vendors that are included in the research. A subscription to that spreadsheet alone is over $150k.

After McGovern's death, the media arm of IDG was sold to a Chinese holding company and the investment arm was sold to McGovern's protégé in China. Since then there have been large scale layoffs at the IDG group of companies.

Yankee

The Yankee Group was founded by Howard Anderson in 1970. It was early to the space and never grew to the extent of a Gartner or Forrester but it was well respected for its thought leadership. It was eventually sold to Primark, a private equity firm, in 1996 for $51 million and then to Reuters for $72.5 million in 2000. It went through more struggles and was eventually sold to the 451 Group at a fire sale.

Forrester Research

Forrester Research was founded by a former Yankee analyst, George Forrester Colony. In its early years it was all about Colony and his research. He was famous for his accurate predictions while at Yankee Group. One such, that the word processing industry would morph into the PC industry, something Wang Computer was probably not happy about, came true. He quit Yankee Group to strike out on his own in 1983 and launched Computing Strategy, which was soon renamed Forrester Research. Colony is a great example of someone who used the influence funnel. He realized the importance of getting quoted in the press.

Forrester went public in 1993 and has acquired several companies including Giga Information Group, Gideon Gartner's second contribution to the research analyst world.

Today, Forrester's 2018 revenue was about $461 million and it has a market cap of $550 million, six weeks into the 2020 market downturn. It employs 1,400 people, a third of which are analysts.

Ovum

Ovum was founded by a tech journalist from the *Sunday Times* in the UK in 1982. After recovering from the tech crash of 2000 it went public on the London Stock Market, AIM, in 2006. It only lasted as a standalone public company until December that year when it was acquired by Datamonitor, which was in turn acquired by a large media holding company, Informa, in 2007. By February of 2020 the Ovum brand was folded into Heavy Reading, an Informa publication, and renamed Omdia. The company claims to have 450 analysts.

451 Research
451 Research was a 20-year-old independent analyst firm. It was acquired by S&P Global Market Intelligence in December 2016 and continues to operate as a separate entity. It employs about 100 industry analysts.

Publishing revolution

Challenge of the Internet
While I was at Gartner, in the aftermath of the dot-com boom but in the early days of the rise of Google, there was a sentiment popping up in the popular press: are Gartner's days numbered? Who needed an analyst firm when a technology buyer could just Google all the information they needed? But Google was sowing the seeds of its own demise as a useful tool for curating information. Google's page rank algorithm encouraged the rise of Search Engine Optimization (SEO), the practice of seeding web content with key words and other tricks to get high placement in search results. You really cannot research an industry on Google. Just try to discover the size of a market using Google. The only results you will find is press releases and quotes that lead back to a prohibitively expensive market research report written by an industry analyst. Since those early claims that industry analyst firms were obsolete, the industry has grown and Gartner's revenue has risen from $858 million in 2003 to $4.25 billion in 2019.

The independents and small firms
It is harder to track the many independent analyst firms. The vast majority consist of only one or two analysts. According to ARInsights, there are over 1,300 analysts firms employing over 7,000 analysts. See Appendix II for a list of the top 100 firms. There is bound to be at least one analyst covering your area of expertise. Seek them out, read their research, decide if you can differentiate your research from theirs. Even if you provide mostly similar services there is always room for more voices.

Duncan Chapple on the Industry Analyst Industry

Duncan Chapple is a consultant on the optimization and valuation of analyst relations. He leads analyst relations services for CCgroup. He is co-director of the Analyst Observatory at the University of Edinburgh Business School. He has directed the two major studies used by analyst relations professionals: the Analyst Value Survey and the Analyst Attitude Survey.

He is the co-author of three books on relationship marketing. Chapple is a co-founder of the Institute for Industry Analyst Relations.

Duncan is the only analyst of industry analysts I know. He provided his thoughts on the business of being an industry analyst below.

Over twenty years, and with tens of millions of datapoints, the Analyst Value Survey has asked professionals what they value from the analysts they use. In parallel, I have spoken to consultants, executives, founders, investors, and sales leaders who have tried to help those firms move forward. What's amazed me is that the demand for analyst insight has intensified year after year, and even during times when technology spending has constricted, such as the 2000 dot-com slump and the 2020 COVID-19 pandemic.

Four distinct stages reflect the several factors that have defined this success.

For much of the late 20th century, we had the "old normal," in which IT followed the business.

In the "dot-com" boom of 1998-2000, IT attempted to be the engine of the business, as enterprises subordinated themselves to centralizing technology stacks that dictated and constrained the evolution of the organization.

The following disruption, in which spending on IT required much deeper business cases, caused employees and managers to start testing out personal or team-wide solutions for business problems.

Today we have a (presumably temporary) equilibrium, a "new normal." Managers outside the IT function directly influence most IT decision making or even determine it.

In each of these stages, the analyst industry has shifted and recomposed itself, extending both its audience and its range of solutions.

I present some of the key findings using the structure of Stephen R. Covey's books on interdependence and effective habits.

1. Be proactive

One of the key differences between market research firms and industry analysts is their bias for action. Market research quantifies the world, in several ways. For industry analysts, however, the point is to change it.

Gartner found that its culture has always been one where brave and challenging positions have been taken. It has produced stalking horses from its very beginning: hypotheses that had to be strong, rather than nuanced or accurate. Analysts have to be challenging and sometimes heroic, but also seem comforting, reassuring, and competent. The future is unknowable. Tech markets often refuse generalization. As a result, analysts can sometimes take very challenging stances.

This can be a difficult balance for any senior analyst. Looking serene, but taking risks, is the classic challenge for organizational leaders in many fields. Analysts have to help clients to suspend their fears so they can start to think about the future and make difficult choices in a more strategic way. Analysts often have difficult relationships with their clients, and not only because of the different needs of buyers and sellers. Sometimes clients have quite unreasonable expectations, and analysts can end up in a surprisingly powerful role. There are no third-party rules, associations, or codes of the type that guide journalists, financial analysts, or PR people.

Perhaps it's that lack of professional standards, or of a professional body of knowledge, but it means that innovation is uneven in the analyst industry. Few firms are proactive, and many copy Gartner. They even copy the aspects of Gartner that are most frustrating.

The big analyst firms look to monetize every interaction: Gartner now demands that even attendees at its updates for analyst relations professionals (which are during Symposium) are open only to ticket holders—even if those people are not actually attending Symposium. The second tier analyst firms are able to grow in niches because their strategy is too difficult for the big firms to imitate: it would liquidate the profits of larger firms, while the smaller firms don't have profits to lose.

End users benefitting from these smaller firms' vendor-funded services are not naïve. Unlike fattening pigs, they understand that since they are not the client, they are to some degree the product. But the growing analyst firms make this into a win-win.

Despite this success, these firms still struggle to monetize fully their strategic success. Many smaller analyst firms have almost no equity value because they depend fully on the personal contacts of the partners. That prevents the firm from developing a growth engine which can survive the departure of the owners. Often tenure is based on high remuneration for business leaders, which erodes profitability.

At the moment these firms have a perhaps temporary advantage caused by the inaction of the largest analyst firms. But they need to monetize and invest increasingly to maintain that advantage. To go to the next level, those firms need to invest in non-analyst executives: especially for marketing, process, sales, and HR development. That allows the firm to build better sales pipelines, client relationships, and client experience.

2. Begin with the end in mind

Too many analyst firms start from the desire to make money from what they know. Far fewer start from the problems of their potential customers, and the expectations of what their customers might have. I've organized several boardroom-form discussions for analysts firms' clients. It's not unusual to hear the same situation described decade after decade:

- When asked what inhibitions vendors faced getting their message across to the analyst community, answers focused around too much choice. Results are that vendors are showing a general lack of knowledge about the analyst world. Navigating the sea of analysts and finding the right individuals for their firms, with knowledge of their industry and needs, is proving difficult.
- Vendors strategically implement information uncovered from research reports and use analyst materials to drive sales and marketing activities. Initiatives cited include competitive intelligence, sales collateral, trend analysis, business planning, market trends, and other areas of value.
- Positive feedback to vendors from customers about mentions in analyst reports was rare. Prospects who refer to analyst feedback on vendors tend to point out any negatives that were discovered.

- A vast majority of vendors surveyed believe that they are not getting the most out of their relationship with analysts. The main reasons listed were lack of resources, time commitment, and lack of communication on behalf of the analyst teams.
- Analysts (including analysts who call themselves consultants or advisors) are often thought to have bias, especially if most of their revenue comes from vendors. Sometimes the effort put into staying informed makes analysts seem very process-driven but less strategic than expected.
- These points represent deep challenges for analyst firms, and especially smaller analyst firms who are especially dependent on vendor support in their early years. Sadly, too many analyst firms focus on evangelizing their analysts' opinions rather than focusing on how to fix the bottlenecks that prevent potential customers in valuing analyst firms.

3. First things first

Like many other professional service firms, the key success factors for analyst firms are salespeople and analysts. Unlike those others firms, however, most analysts restrict themselves to hiring experienced professionals.

In the report of our successful academic research project into analysts' career vectors, my co-authors and I found that larger analyst firms tend to hire senior analysts from industry and from competitors rather than train people up from their early careers. Unlike many other professional services firms, analysts need to hit the ground running. As in other fields where people are thrown in at the deep end, impostor syndrome can be common.

Strong professional standards and ethical policies are even more important because vendors' subscriptions to analyst firms can look like a conflict of interests. Vendor support for the analyst community is substantial: many obtain more revenue from vendors than from users. Most analyst houses cannot have their opinions bought, but few have clear policies to help explain it. Uncritical research stands out sharply and will often be discounted by people planning technology investments.

Here are five policies that I think most analyst firms should consider:
- Organizationally separate any commercial relationships with vendors from its findings.
- Do not in any way tie its findings or its research coverage to the absence or presence of a commercial relationship.

- Do not withhold research coverage due to the absence of a commercial relationship.
- Research personnel shall not be influenced by sales personnel or by management personnel with the intent of directing or influencing specific research findings for financial gain.

To the extent that any special products or services are developed which are sponsored by vendors either directly or indirectly, such sponsorship shall be disclosed explicitly in a fashion physically proximate to the research.

The lack of such clear policies has meant that some vendors are standoffish about analysts. In particular, some vendors have found an issue with smaller analyst firms or those focused on marketing. They can get into a cycle where the analyst is focused on how the vendor can improve its rhetoric and slides, and the more the vendor follows the analyst's advice, the better the feedback gets—even though no real change has happened in the company or its standing in the market.

4. Think win-win

One of the biggest struggles in my work is trying to convince technology companies that analyst influence cannot be bought. Especially in smaller firms, they don't see analyst firms as having a win-win attitude. The biggest obstacle to clients building win-win relationships with analyst firms is the pay-to-play idea that analysts firms' outcomes reflect the commercial relationships they have with vendors.

Greg Wind, an analyst relations consultant, gives two examples of the scenarios where people get suspicious of analyst firms. "The first is fairly straightforward: a salesperson, or even the analyst you're meeting with, stops the conversation to discuss the various paid services they offer, including white papers, case studies, vendor profiles, etc. (...)

"The second is less clear, but important to consider in this context: the case of the very persuasive account manager. This is the person who makes things happen—pushes for that briefing the analyst declined, works you into a report you might have been excluded from, or helps to minimize bad coverage."

Independence is one of the most important things that buyers from analysts firms want, and it's one of the things they are most concerned about. We make a point of asking about it in the Analyst Value Survey. Analysts' clients are the people who are best able to make an informed judgment about the relative independence of these leading analyst firms, and there's no more effective alternative to a survey. One surprise we've had: the more people there are commenting on a firm, the more independent the firm is. Perhaps that means that the more eyes there are on a firm, the more careful it is about its independence.

5. Seek first to understand, then to be understood

As analyst firms grow, their division of labor becomes more granular and narrow. However, the groups of executives who decide on technology investments (what we call buying centers) are getting larger. That produces a pressure. Executives want analyst insight to be more joined up and integrated, but it instead becomes more focused.

Many niche players write about horizontal trends, but they struggle to do so either deeply, to meet the needs of managers, or strategically, to provide content that helps managers to make the case for change. Few analyst firms take up the opportunity to develop joint research programs with horizontal specialists (imagine, for example, Celent or Aite developing a joint service with BARC, the leading analytics boutique). We also note that, on the supply side, many professionals who work for vendors and providers that consume research on fintech also have an interest in healthcare, which faces some similar issues about regulation, identity, B2B onboarding, auditing, and the data supply chain. Niche firms could leverage expertise in similar markets which might have experiences and use cases that are powerful guides in their own markets. Clearly, vendors' analyst relations teams can play a role here by reaching out to vertical analysts with relevant use cases for horizontal technologies.

6. Synergize!

The growth of freemium services has been key to the explosive growth of the analyst firms. Analyst firms have both a classic freemium model, where buyers can consume limited research but pay for the most valuable content, and a vendor-supported model where the premium is paid by vendors, leaving much of the research free to consume. While this leads to revenue for analyst firms, the truth is that premium customers get more value.

Freemium users are those who are not paying for the research they consume from the firm, whether because of classic freemium (most content is initially free, and some pay for later services) or because of reprints paid for by vendors. For example, around a quarter of the people who use Aite or Celent say their organization has a subscription to it, but most of those people do say their organizations subscribe to Gartner and Forrester. That means the average user gets less value because they have less access to the full range of services.

Freemium isn't the only way to broaden the audience for analyst firms. When I was an analyst and shareholder at Ovum, the largest European firm and the fourth-largest worldwide, I was amazed by the turn-around in our appeal to clients and investors that came from increasing our investment in media relations. Speaking for the firm on TV and radio had an international impact.

I regularly make regional analyses of analyst firms' media profiles to see which firms are enhancing their coverage. One surprise is many analyst firms are mentioned more in EMEA than they are in the Americas. Part of that is having firms like TechMarketView and Omdia, which have European roots, but our research showed that Gartner was mentioned more in the EMEA media than in the US media. Gartner does well in Asia-Pacific too, where it, IDC, Frost & Sullivan, and Informa (which includes Omdia) are very often cited. Furthermore, the region has some firms that have a higher share of voice in Asia-Pacific than in other areas, such as Greyhound, Canalys and AMI Partners.

7. Sharpen the Saw: Growth

A huge part of Gartner's initial success was Theory G, the firm's understanding that excellence isn't static. Gideon Gartner explains:

Theory G may sound trite but the idea was to emphasize our continuing need for excellence, that we were in business to serve clients and that clients were people first (not companies). Its simplistic list of do's and don'ts included: be enthusiastic, self-critical, proponents of change, contribute and share across the firm, and so forth. It might have sounded corny to some but I hoped that when and if our employees dug deeper into the theory, they would recognize a process which included research directives such as: correct errors of fact immediately, advocate positions explicitly, improve abilities to sell a specific point of view, and optimize the way time was spent when working! Some claimed these directions were simply 'motherhood,' but we nevertheless took time to formalize our views with regard to increasing confidence in our values and beating our competitors.

8. Find your voice and inspire others to find theirs

Over the years, many users of analysts' services are reporting to the Analyst Value Survey much higher satisfaction with firms that are seen as being more interactive, community-oriented, and engaging. Alsbridge, HFS Research, and ISG have been often mentioned as examples. Indeed, it's fair to say that we see real enthusiasm from both suppliers and enterprises that there are now really promising complimentary providers, which are more inspiring than Gartner or IDC.

We also see the impact of free research. Many respondents are in firms that have limited their number of employees able to access the major analyst houses, producing the intriguing scenario that free research might be used more widely in some organizations than the analyst firms it subscribes to. It is now possible to be an expert user of analysts, and to know the analysts and their firms well, but not actually have seat to a subscription. Generally, of course, most respondents are in organizations that are Gartner subscribers, but as individuals they might not have access. Certainly, we are seeing Gartner's monopoly on a premium customer experience is slipping. There are many firms that seriously compete with Gartner when it comes to finding ways of understanding the world and helping their own organizations to articulate a way forward.

That shift towards firms' using a plurality of analyst insight providers is especially driven by the development of cloud solutions and outsourcing services across the entire IT and telecoms world. Services analysts and sourcing advisors seem to have a finger in every pie. As one AVS respondent explained, "The challenge that both the analysts and the advisory firms have is the broad rapidly changing technology in the marketplace. The decision they have to make is to limit their focus or grow their practice in order to cover all of these areas." That seems to be pushing people to refine their investment in analyst firms in two ways: either to identify individual analysts rather than firms to have strategic relationships with; or to find one firm that can cover all their needs.

Of course the more extensive coverage of the market by Gartner, Forrester, and IDC is not their only advantage. Gartner, for example, has three sales people for every analyst: a ratio that other analyst firms would be well advised to follow. A wide range of coverage areas isn't always better for every client, especially if you have a question that three of four analysts have different parts of the answer to, leaving you to make sense of them.

It would be mistaken to think that the other analyst firms that are performing well in the Analyst Value Survey are all getting the same things right. A great illustration of that is the list of analyst firms we are most likely to add into the survey next year (we're too polite to talk about the ones they will replace, especially since many of those are respected national leaders with little regional or global traction). While we aim to include in the survey every firm with more than a dozen full-time analysts, we see that there are some smaller firms that have a notable level of market impact. TechMarketView is a great example of that. We are also seeing firms with more innovative business models, like

BI Intelligence, and with niche leadership, like insurance analysts Novarica. Gartner's leadership in market share will be hard to erode while it continues not only to have sales leadership, but also deliver better value for the money than other large analyst firms.

How to Be a Curmudgeon

The word curmudgeon has negative connotations. It is usually associated with a grumpy, asocial downer. My dictionary defines curmudgeon as "an avaricious, churlish fellow, a miser." There are other interpretations of the word that are more charitable. In the context of an industry analyst, and perhaps the Gartner legacy, a curmudgeon is a contrarian, somebody who questions authoritative opinions, an iconoclast. If he or she also displays a dry wit and has a pithy way with words, all the better.

In his introduction to *The Portable Curmudgeon*, Jon Winokur defends curmudgeons:

> A curmudgeon's reputation for malevolence is undeserved. They're neither warped nor evil at heart. They don't hate mankind, just mankind's excesses. They're just as sensitive and softhearted as the next guy, but they hide their vulnerability beneath a crust of misanthropy. They ease the pain by turning hurt into humor. They snarl at pretense and bite at hypocrisy.

Where do you look for things to be curmudgeonly about? Everywhere. Here are just a few places to look:

- Earnings calls and press releases from public companies. Usually the words out of a CEO's mouth have been carefully scrubbed by a host of marketing and legal people. Invariably the words are twisted to put the company's strategy in the best possible light, often with glaring holes in the logic.
- Funding and M&A announcements. When WeWork was valued at over $7 billion, a curmudgeon would have been calling out the holes in the CEOs claims. She would have questioned a company that invested in long term leases while earning revenue from short term leases. Although nobody did, it would have established an analyst as a mage if he or she

had questioned how that model could survive an economic downturn, or even a global pandemic that put everyone under a shelter-at-home order.
- M&A announcements are an excellent opportunity to provide curmudgeonly commentary. Question the strategic arguments put forth by the acquirer. Will there really be synergies, as claimed? Are there underlying business reasons that those claimed synergies will never materialize? In my space, the IT security industry, there are many examples. Symantec, the largest anti-virus company at the time, acquired a data center software company, Veritas, in 2004 for $13.5 billion. It was easy to be opposed to what was the largest tech acquisition of the time, and be proved right when Symantec spun Veritas back out to private equity in 2015 for $8 billion. Or the ridiculous strategy put forward by the leadership of Intel for acquiring another AV vendor, McAfee, in 2010 for $7.68 billion. Another deal that was a disaster for everyone involved.
- Ask yourself, what does this proposed deal/investment mean for the industry? For the investors? For the employees? And for the customers? Don't just criticize, offer advice for how to make the best of a bad situation.
- Read the prognostication of other analysts covering your space. Do you agree? Do you violently disagree? Go ahead and publish your take. It's always good to have a contrary opinion to the Gartner or Forrester analyst. Don't expect them to come back at you. They are the ones standing on the stage. They don't need to acknowledge your existence.
- Don't become a broken record. Don't latch on to a theme and keep harping on it.
- Twitter. Create your own curated list of people who speak out and write about your industry. Tune in daily and contribute your thoughts. Sometimes you can pick up on a growing consensus around a topic on Twitter. Question that. Understand what makes people believe a certain thing. "Never write down passwords!" Then write about why that is wrong. You might not want to engage in debates on Twitter, get your ideas there.
- Challenge a vendor during a briefing. Many vendors pick up on the common themes of the industry or regurgitate the research of Gartner or even dodgy reports out of pay-to-play research firms. Question the vendor's claims. Push back on their strategy. Offer a different view. But be respectful.

- Comment on breaking news. The companies you follow will inevitably be in the news. Write about the news but bring your unique vision. Don't contribute to the choir of responses if everyone is expressing the same view. Raise alternative explanations and analysis.
- Support the new at the expense of the old.

How to Become an Analyst

There are two primary routes to becoming an industry analyst. The first, and most common, is to join an existing analyst firm. This chapter will suggest the avenues to accomplishing that goal before moving on to the transition to private practice and becoming an independent analyst. There are also opportunities for skipping the established firm route and building a reputation that allows you to go solo right from the start.

The large firms have the ability to anoint new analysts. From time to time they have experimented with growing their own from scratch. Gartner once made a practice of hiring journalism graduates directly into their analyst programs. I guess the idea was that finding industry experts and retaining them was too haphazard. People with the communication skills and industry expertise were already gainfully employed. They were also very expensive to hire away from industry. Some of those journo-analysts became very effective analysts and went on to be extremely influential in their fields, commanding top salaries in industry. One I worked closely with holds the top strategy position at a major network security company.

Today the analyst firms tend to focus on hiring people that are already familiar with the industries they are hired to cover. The preference is for people who have worked in large organizations such as those that comprise the analyst firm's client base. In this way the hiring firm can be comfortable that the analyst can "talk the talk" of their customers. The hardest thing to select for in recruiting though is vision. Because of this, many analysts have a world view that is frozen in the paradigms of their time as a practitioner.

Getting hired into a major firm can take several paths. The straightest path is to monitor their career sites:

Gartner: jobs.gartner.com/
Forrester: go.forrester.com/careers/
IDC: www.idc.com/about/careers

Omdia: informacareers.silkroad.com/
451 Research: 451research.com/about-us/our-company/careers

Many positions are also posted to LinkedIn. Use the "search by company" function to find them.

When an analyst position is posted, do not apply directly! Get an internal advocate to put your name forward. If you have been in the field for at least five years you probably already have a personal contact at the analyst firm. If you do not, reach out on LinkedIn with a request to connect. Or, engage an analyst in an email exchange, even a politely worded request to forward your resume to HR. Gartner in particular pays a reported $4,000 to employees that provide a resume of a successful candidate.

What should your resume look like? It should demonstrate that you have the traits listed in Chapter One. That means a technical degree, work experience in the field you are applying to cover, and demonstrated communication skills. Having a published book on just about any topic would be one of the best qualifications. If it is in your field, that is even better. Experience presenting at major conferences is great. It demonstrates that you are already recognized in the space. If you are a prolific blogger on your industry, you will get noticed. If your blog posts are analytical and filled with actionable advice, you will most probably get an immediate response from the internal recruiters.

Which role should you apply for? Each analyst firm has different roles and hierarchies. At Gartner there are two divisions of analysts: the traditional Gartner analysts, and the team that is derived from the Burton Group acquisition. The Burton Group analysts are much more practical in their coverage and topics, whereas the mainstream Gartner analysts are meant to be thought leaders. Frankly, you should shoot for the latter, although going the Burton Group route may be a way to get in the door. But, as you most likely already have learned, the best time to negotiate your position and salary is during the hiring process. Once you are in the door you have to follow the established paths to advance. Always aim high.

Gartner is worse than a bank when it comes to titles. The top title for an analyst is VP Research. The VP is rarely spelled out. It is almost as if it could stand for Venerated Person rather than Vice President. The other titles are Analyst, Senior Analyst and Director. There is an additional designation of Distinguished Analyst, which is usually earned after years of continuous service at Gartner.

Let me describe my own experience getting hired into Gartner in 2000. It was the end of the dot-com boom and I was winding down a failed startup in the online gift certificate business that I had built for a PwC client. I was working with three other startups whose founders all promised a CEO position "as soon as they got funding." Of course, they expected me to help them get that funding.

Earlier in the dot-com boom I had submitted my resume to the website of one of the major headhunting firms. I had listed my experience as a Check Point Software reseller and a manager of Technical Risk Services at PricewaterhouseCoopers (where I ran their firewall lab) in my resume, so when the recruiter got a request from Gartner for someone with firewall experience, they called me.

I was only vaguely familiar with Gartner at the time. I had used their research while at PwC. The hiring manager, Bob Hafner, headed up the networking practice. His one network security analyst, John Pescatore, was completely swamped. Clients that were calling to schedule inquiries with JP were being put off for 6-8 weeks. They needed someone who was familiar with the firewall space to take some of the load off of him.

After a couple of phone conversations with Hafner and JP, they scheduled a time for me to visit 56 Top Gallant Road on the shores of Stamford, Connecticut. They sent a stretch limousine to LaGuardia to pick me up. When I was dropped off at the lobby of Gartner's headquarters, I was met by an internal recruiter who coached me in the process. I was to retire to a room for a couple of hours and write a research report on one of three topics they had sent me. Then I was to sit with Hafner and several of the analysts and present my findings. At which point I was warned the Gartner analysts would grill me. The recruiter warned me several times DO NOT BACK DOWN. Stick to my guns at all costs.

Well, she put me in a room under the stairway with a desk and an old IBM PC and left me to write. The topic was on which VPN technology would win out in the marketplace. After two hours I was led up to a conference room where four local analysts were present and an additional three or four were dialed in on a conference call. I presented my findings and they started to grill me. Within the hour I backed down. They convinced me I was wrong. I failed. I was not analyst material.

The recruiter led me to the lobby and told me they would be in touch. I had to call a city cab to take me back to the airport. Not a good interview experience.

They did call though. The recruiter was upbeat, only the offer was for Senior Analyst, not for the posted position of Director. I was not too concerned about the bait and switch on the title, what about the money? The offer was not even close to my already-communicated minimum base. I told her thanks but no thanks. A quick follow up call from Bob Hafner to confirm that my only problem was financial and that was the last I ever expected to hear from Gartner.

Three months later I was getting off a plane on my return from visiting one of those startups that hoped would make me their CEO when I got the call from the recruiter: The position was still open and I was the best candidate they had talked to. Ka-ching! Fist pump.

Two weeks later I was at Disney World for Gartner's huge IT Symposium event. Within a month my backlog of client calls matched Pescatore's.

You will notice that I did not have many of the qualifications I listed earlier. Most of my experience with writing came from creating business plans for startups and project proposals for PwC. I had never held an IT job. Sure, I had worked with the founders of the major firewall vendor when they were still a small company. I had run a security lab for PwC and participated in attack and penetration testing at some of the largest companies in the world. No way was I a subject matter expert. But I did have that insatiable thirst for knowledge. In school I would neglect my studies to spend hours roaming the stacks at the University of Michigan libraries researching topics that were of more interest than circuits or thermodynamics. I started an ISP in 1993 because it gave me access to the Internet where the world's knowledge was available through surfing using tools like Archie, Veronica, and WAIS. I thought I was cut out to be an entrepreneur when I was actually exhibiting the traits of an industry analyst. I started seventeen companies, most of them failures. The ensuing four years I spent at Gartner was the longest period I have ever been an employee.

Life as a Gartner analyst

Let me continue the autobiographical thread by painting a picture of life as an analyst at Gartner. From my conversations with analyst friends at Forrester, Yankee, and IDC, I gather that while the products and mix of activities are different, overall the experience is similar.

Gartner has a three day Boot Camp they put me through to expose me to their methodologies. They introduced the concept of a Stalking Horse and the various forms of reports they created. A Stalking Horse is a trial run at a new research thesis. It is written up and circulated internally to be torn down by other analysts, or approved with enhancements. They also taught the new recruits how to use the probabilities assigned to predictions. You have seen those: "By 2020 all computing will be done in the cloud (P 0.3)." That's a 30% confidence level in the prediction. "There will be a significant breach of security within critical infrastructure before 2019 (P 0.9)." That's a high probability of 90%.

It took only a couple of months to be fully immersed in the life of a Gartner analyst. Each analyst is required to designate four or more open slots in each day's calendar for client inquiries. A huge call center receives those inquiries, matches them up with the appropriate analyst, and schedules it on your calendar. Invariably the call center has to reach out to get you to open more time slots because your week is already booked solid.

When I was not traveling I would be up and ready for the first call at 9:00 a.m.. It was usually with the CIO and his or her team. They would have specific questions that could have anything at all to do with security. Products, companies, people, methodologies, processes, certifications—anything. I learned to respond in fifteen minute mini-lectures. To this day, I have trouble being brief. After two questions were addressed, it was on to the next call. In the early months this was an extremely stressful occupation. I was on the spot, sometimes talking to people who knew a lot more about what they were doing than I did. But after six months it became rare to encounter a new question. They were always the same. And now I had the composite experience of hundreds of similar IT departments with the same questions. I was becoming an expert. I knew the answers. I knew them so well that there was no embarrassment when I encountered a question I could not answer. That is a powerful feeling.

But fielding client inquiries is only a small part of an analyst's duties. There are also:

Vendor briefings. Every analyst learns to dread briefings. It is not unusual to sit through eight vendor briefings a week. Each hour-long session invariably means going through a PowerPoint presentation that describes the problem and the wonderful solution that the vendor provides. In security it seemed that every vendor had a circle diagram to describe the monitor-detect-fix-update-monitor cycle of their product. I even kept a collection of these.

No matter the drudgery, vendor briefings are valuable. The vendors are the ones pushing the envelope and they usually have just as many, if not far more, interactions with end users as an analyst. What they are seeing in the space gets reflected in their products. Being fully conversant with all of the product solutions available is a key requirement for any industry analyst.

Conferences. Gartner has over 45 different events every year, from the week-long Fall and Spring Symposia to the specific topic areas in each technology sector. An analyst is expected to participate in the conferences dedicated to their topic. This means preparing and presenting a "pitch." These presentations are given a lot of weight in evaluating an analyst and conference attendees hang on every word. Planning for events starts six months prior and all slide decks have to be ready at least a month in advance. Pescatore and I used to each take one side of the security dichotomy. One of us would address the rising threats, the other would address the state of the art in defense. One year we got to Symposium and at the last minute JP said, "Let me look at your slides." Sure enough I had used the same slides as he had! Forty-five minutes before I went on stage I was frantically assembling new slides, but it went off without a hitch. After that I tended to treat deadlines as soft targets. It was also at these conferences that I learned some of the secrets to good presentations. Hafner was the one who told me to inject more energy. Like many neophyte presenters I was so concerned about content that I tended to drone on a bit. I have since learned to keep it upbeat and most importantly to build a story into a presentation. Much more on presentations later.

Symposium is a massive event with close to 10,000 attendees from the Gartner client base and over 150 vendors with booths in the Exposition area. It is a week-long extravaganza of keynotes from the CEOs of top technology firms. Bill Gates, Steve Balmer, Steve Jobs, and Larry Ellison have all been on the main stage at Symposium. Each analyst has several sessions to present as well as grueling hours in booths doing one-on-one meetings with vendors and end users.

The one-on-ones. At every Gartner event attendees have an opportunity to meet with the analyst one-on-one. It's a live inquiry. For the client it is extremely valuable to get what Pescatore calls "high bandwidth connection" with the analyst. For the analyst, the 4-6 hours spent in the rat maze of temporary booths set up in the noisy one-on-one hall is pure torture. No sooner are you done talking to the client from Columbia about banking infrastructure when the next client is ushered into your presence to talk about how to set up a security team, or which vendor product is better for X.

Sales calls. Each Gartner analyst is expected to join a sales team at least one day a quarter. The sales team is tasked with demonstrating value to their customers, especially right before it comes time to renew their annual contracts. One way to do this is to bring the analyst by for a chat. For the analyst it means a day of driving from client to client, sometimes literally being dropped by the side of the road for another member of the sales team to pick you up for the next appointment. One skill I learned from these experiences was to always remember where the sales person had parked. I noticed early on that they were so rushed and so focused on making a good impression on me that they forgot where they left their car. After the 3rd or 4th time walking up and down parking structures I always made a mental note of the car's location when we parked; a valuable life skill.

Research reports. Every analyst firm has a set of reports to get out. The most important and influential of all reports is the Gartner Magic Quadrant.

Here is how Magic Quadrants are created, based on my four years as the primary author of two Magic Quadrants and secondary author on several more. It is also derived from my knowledge of changes to the process since I left. Thanks to frequent challenges to their process and objectivity from disgruntled vendors, Gartner has put a lot of work into improving their methodology. I also work with many vendors on their responses to the surveys Gartner sends out for Magic Quadrants so I have seen this evolution first hand. If you are going to be a Gartner analyst, let this description serve as a warning for what you are about to get into.

Each Magic Quadrant has at least one primary author and possibly several secondary authors depending on the size and importance of a product category. The responsibility for creating an MQ is the most onerous task a Gartner Analyst has. (Creating 18-slide PowerPoint presentations for Summits and Symposia is the next most onerous task.) Analysts dread the process. They like to be thinking about and researching the next big thing, not re-hashing ground they covered over and over.

In most cases, the MQ for a particular category already exists. The analyst either was present at the inception or inherited the MQ from another analyst who has moved up, moved on to other areas of coverage, or left Gartner altogether. There is surprisingly little support structure at Gartner—no research assistants, secretaries, fact checkers, or Business Intelligence tools to help them. There is a huge staff of editors but they are often a hindrance, not a help. Gartner editors make sure that Research Notes are in the "Gartner voice," thus eliminating the opportunity for an analyst to imbue his or her research with his own voice and flavor of discourse. Gartner analysts are individual contributors and remarkably free from the day-to-day hassles you would expect from a highly paid professional, often with the title of Vice President. They have no direct-reports, thus no employee evaluations to fill out, and few meetings, except by conference call to discuss research agendas and coordinate Summit activities. They work from home and are often on the road. Other than producing Research Notes and presentations, the vast majority of their time is taken up with briefings and inquiries—predominantly over the phone.

The publication of MQs used to be scheduled to coincide with the Gartner IT Symposium at Disney World every fall, but today that is not adhered to as strictly. Their presentations are supposed to include updated Magic Quadrants for their sectors. Often the official schedule for MQs is for a new one to appear every six months. Because of the tremendous work load, this often gets collapsed into one every twelve months, which is actually a blessing for the vendors. Responding to the MQ surveys is an arduous task, too.

First the analyst must decide who makes the cut for the next version of the MQ. They look at all the vendors who have been acquired or, thanks to their inside knowledge, are about to be acquired. They determine what the inclusion criteria will be, often a gross revenue measure but sometimes a new requirement based on changes to the market. Throughout the year they would have been making notes about new vendors to include, usually as niche vendors, based on the 200-400 vendor briefings they have participated in.

The analyst then refines the spreadsheet containing the 20-150 questions that are going to be used to generate the positions in the Magic Quadrant. In addition to the actual questions, they come up with the secret weightings that are applied to each answer from each vendor. The questionnaires are usually broken down into business questions and product capability questions that line up with the Ability to Execute and Completeness of Vision axes.

The analyst must then send the questionnaire to the contact person on record at each vendor. This is the part they dread. It is the official kick-off of the vendor response cycle. Savvy vendors use this phase to schedule briefings and inquiries (if they are clients) to get clarification on what the analyst is thinking. It could mean fifteen or more scheduled calls for the analyst, all to discuss the upcoming MQ.

When the vendors respond by the required time, with the usual pleas for extensions, the responses are reviewed and combined into one spreadsheet. A score, or rating, is given to each answer, and each question has a weight associated with it: low-standard-high. At the press of a button the ratings and weights are applied and the Magic Quadrant is created! Well, that is how it would work in an ideal world. In reality, each vendor responds with different units, different time scales (oh, you meant calendar quarters!), and often just confusing entries. The analyst has to determine if the reported revenue is bookings, sales, or even if the vendor pulled some slight-of-hand reporting list price sales instead of discounted sales, or whether they bundle services and consulting into product revenue. It's a nightmare.

Once all the data is normalized and perhaps adjusted to reflect reality, an MQ is generated. Now comes the subjective part. The spreadsheet tool may cluster all the respective dots from all the vendors around the crosshairs—all the vendors are almost the same in ability to execute and completeness of vision. No problem, the scale is adjusted to spread them out. Then the analyst does a reality check. Does that vendor with the slick product but only 25 employees really belong in the Leaders Quadrant? Is IBM really a niche vendor in the space? How did the company that was first to market fall below the line into

Visionary? How has the picture changed from the year before—can the major moves be explained?

After all the adjustments, and a review by the other analysts to get buy-in, the draft MQ is sent to all the participating vendors along with the brief synopsis of their company and product that will be in the main body of the research note. Then the fun begins. Every vendor who is not happy with their placement makes urgent requests for briefings to clarify their position or argue why they are so much better than the vendors ranked above them. Even the vendors placed in the Leaders Quadrant will not be happy unless they are the farthest UP and to the RIGHT. Every word of the synopsis will be scrutinized by the vendor and they will lobby for minor changes that portray them in a better light. Vendors have been known to count the number of words devoted to them and attempt to bring that number in line with their competitors' count.

Finally the analyst will complete the vendor response phase and send the MQ off to editing, where it is scrubbed for language compliance and formatted for publication. It is out of the analyst's hands. She breathes a sigh of relief and moves on to the other MQ for which she is responsible.

Today an analyst may devote as much as 300 hours to creating and publishing a Magic Quadrant. If you do go to work at Gartner, consider yourself warned.

SAS days. Gartner and many other firms will hire out their analysts for day-long strategy sessions. The most fun and productive are the rare occasion when this is for an end user client. Most of the time, these Strategic Advisory Services (SAS) days are with vendors. The analyst flies out, stays in a hotel, drives to the vendor site, and spends a day getting completely briefed on the vendor's products, services, sales strategy, marketing plans, and future developments. The vendor gets value out of the time spent, first by hopefully influencing the analyst to think positively about them, and second from the strategic advice the analyst gives. Gartner used to pay the analyst a bonus of a couple hundred dollars for each day (for which they charged the vendor $12,000), but today there are no financial benefits to the analyst for SAS days. I used to do 50 SAS days a year. That is one of the things that got me thinking about being on my own. 50 x $12k = $600k! Not bad work if you can get it. More on how to get that work later. The fee today for an analyst day is closer to $25,000.

Occupational hazards of being an analyst

With these tasks you can see that being an analyst entails a lot "hats" as Bob Hafner calls them. The compensation can be good but the work schedule is grueling. There are two occupational hazards to be aware of: divorce and health. With the busy schedule and high demand on your time that could involve late night calls from anywhere in the world, and all that travel, keeping a strong marriage is a challenge. Make sure your spouse or soon-to-be spouse knows what to expect before you dive in.

You may also have noticed that the only aspects of the analyst job that I have mentioned so far that do not involve sitting down is presenting at conferences and running behind a salesperson on the four days a year that you do sales calls. All the rest of the time you are sitting at your desk or on the couch or in an airplane. This is called a sedentary life style and you may notice it is reflected in the waist line of most of the analysts you meet. Travel means eating in restaurants a lot, quite often good restaurants with good wine. While it sounds attractive, it is a dangerous occupation.

On the health front just watch what you eat. Your primary exercise is going to come from walking between gates. I gained 50 pounds over the years. Luckily, I figured out I was eating too many carbs. I cut those out and lost the 50 pounds.

Now that we have looked at getting a job at a major analyst firm and what it is like to work there, let's address the next steps.

Leaving Gartner

Turnover at the major firms, especially Gartner, is low. Why after all would someone leave at the top of their game? How often does a major league baseball player bow out mid-career to take a job as a sportscaster or manager? A Gartner analyst is at the top of the pyramid. Their every statement is listened to. They move markets. They push vendors to be better. Their advice saves clients millions.

I left because I was bored. It had gotten to the point where I would no longer read the questions I was about to address before I called in to client conference calls. The uncertainty and the hope that I would get a new question added a little flavor to the day. I only lasted four years. There was also the matter of money. You cannot get rich as a Gartner analyst. There is also the frustration of dealing with the editorial review process. Gartner's editing team erases your voice. How can you derive satisfaction from writing if you do not recognize your own words when they are published?

I have only witnessed one exit route for analysts. They have strongly worded twelve month non-compete contracts that prevent them from joining a competitor or going out on their own. So, they join vendors. The most common role is VP of Strategy. Occasionally they take on the job of analyst relations where they are responsible for influencing analysts to write about and give high marks to their product. Sometimes they take marketing roles. I took a job as an evangelist for a software security company that had gone from zero to $100 million in revenue in a few years. They were a surefire IPO about to happen. Sadly, their product sales were to consumers and they never managed to break into the enterprise space. On top of that, their sales flattened out and they never went public.

But as an evangelist I got to continue to work with the press and travel the world speaking at conferences. I was working on my analyst skills. By 2005 I was ready to leave, my non-compete with Gartner had expired, and I thought I had a great idea for re-inventing the analyst business. So I went out on my own and launched IT-Harvest.

Here was my big idea: create a database of all the vendors in my space and sell subscriptions to access that data with a great cloud-based web front end. But a funny thing happened along the way. We invested over $35k in building an interactive tool for querying the database. We built a backend so that the work-from-home research assistants we hired could quickly and easily populate the tool with data. And we began to sell subscriptions for $5,000/year. Not a single subscriber ever logged in to the tool. What they were buying was access to me, the analyst. Our sales guy had pitched the subscription with bundled access to me. That's what the customers wanted and were willing to pay for. We had reinvented the wheel. This is exactly how all analyst firms operate. Clients don't necessarily want the information: they want, and value, access to the expert.

But I have left a question unanswered. How do you become an industry analyst without doing time at a major firm first?

There are no degree programs, certifying bodies, or online classes in industry analysis. There are no industry analyst professional societies, not even a trade guild. I like to compare becoming a professional analyst to becoming a professional tradesman. When I was in high school I enjoyed shop class, especially welding; so much so that I enrolled in night school to take more classes in welding. I even took a summer school class at my State University in joining and welding of materials. I leveraged those classes and the slight skills I picked up to get a job in a ship yard in Northern Wisconsin as a welder. It took three days of intensive training in a welding lab built in an old freighter to acquire the skills I needed to be put to work on a 1,000-foot ore carrier. I only worked one summer in the ship yard between years at college, but I learned lessons I took with me to my career as an automotive engineer. If I had spent five years as a welder, I would have become an expert. I could have risen through the ranks at the ship yard or I could have started my own fabrication business. This is the same choice anyone who is proficient at a trade has. An analyst comes up through the ranks.

Here are three paths to becoming an industry analyst. All of them start with the five or more years it takes to gain proficiency in your sector. You have to know what makes your industry tick, or at least know a piece of the puzzle.

Path 1. Get hired by an analyst firm.

This is the most direct route. Identify the firms that you think you would like to work at. Get to know the analysts that cover your space. Follow them on Twitter and LinkedIn. Go to their presentations or attend their webinars. Continue to build your expertise in your field. Keep an eye on job postings. Set up a job alert on LinkedIn. Start applying. Alert the analysts you know. They may even put your name forward as a candidate. Often they are compensated for finding new hires.

I was very lucky to get hired by Gartner. It was at the tail end of the dot-com boom and I had filled out a profile at one of the big headhunting firms. I was winding up a failed startup in 2000 and looking for the next thing. I was only vaguely aware of Gartner. I had used their Dataquest research when I was at PricewaterhouseCoopers.

Other than getting recruited directly, as I did, the best route is to make connections within analyst firms. Write about your space. Several analysts I know wrote a book on their space before getting hired. When you see an opening, reach out to those connections. Work your network.

Path 2. Build an analyst function for somebody else.

The best way to be an entrepreneur I have encountered is to not actually strike off on your own, but to build your new idea at your current employer. If you have an idea that you think could be a success, a money maker, or fill a gap in the offerings of your company, build it for them. You get the same fun of creating a business plan and pitching it to investors (your boss, the CEO, the Board), but you have the support structure of accounting, HR, sales, and marketing. So think how an analyst function within your organization could enhance its offerings. Do you work for a manufacturer? Think how a competitive analysis department could evolve into a way to publish research, establishing your company (and you) as the experts in the field. Gideon Gartner did that within the company he worked for. Check out the guidance provided by Priceonomics.com on how to use the data already at hand to create value for your organization.

This is a great way to morph into an industry analyst without having to get hired by a big firm or face the challenges of striking out on your own. Your salary and benefits are covered. You can expense your flights to meet customers or attend conferences. And, most importantly, you do not need to save up a cushion of financial reserves.

Path 3. Strike out on your own.

Think long and hard about this one. Going it alone is risky. All of the traits I listed that make a good analyst do not include the traits of someone that is comfortable without a safety net, willing to risk it all, happy to manage accounting, sales, collections, marketing, etc. Doing all the tasks of launching a business takes away from the tasks of an analyst: thinking, reading, researching, and writing.

Often the impetus to create your own firm is provided by circumstances. You may already be an analyst at a big firm but you get laid off. Or you are an industry expert who gets laid off or retires after a long career. In order to start your own business you need two things: time and money. To quote my older brother, you rarely have both. But losing your job provides you with one of those. If you have savings, a health insurance plan continued from your employer (COBRA in the US), and possibly a spouse who is gainfully employed, then this may be your chance.

It can take six months or more to find a new job, so why not build up a practice in that time frame? Getting laid off might mean that there is also an economic downturn so jobs are hard to find. If you are over 55 it may be difficult finding a job at all. It is a sad reality that employers shy away from hiring older workers.

The upside of starting your own firm is the long term stability. You have flexibility to adjust your products and offerings to accommodate changing markets. You end up having your dream job, calling the shots, and generating multiple revenue streams. How can anyone be afraid of hard work doing what they love?

Whichever path you choose, the next chapter will help you on your way.

The Analyst Path

While it is possible to become an acknowledged expert in any field you choose, it is probably wisest to put a little thought into how you can get from where you are today to where you need to be. You may already be well along the way to becoming an expert.

If you have the traits listed in Chapter One, you have probably already achieved many of the steps below. The easiest metric to determine if you are ready to become an independent analyst is the 10,000 hour rule made popular by Malcolm Gladwell in his book *Outliers: The Story of Success*. After introducing us to studies conducted by K. Anders Ericsson, who surveyed violinists and pianists, Gladwell concludes: "Ten thousand hours is the magic number of greatness." He goes on to demonstrate how this rule holds true for many fields.

Before jumping into the specifics of creating the persona of an expert, there are some things to keep in mind. You must approach all of the steps below with the mindset of an analyst—before you have learned that mindset. Keep in mind the following:

1. Always have an opinion. You are not a journalist, you are an analyst. This can be a hard transition to make for someone who is a journalist. Even a corporate environment can train people to couch their recommendations in a passive, wishy-washy voice. It is self-preservation when you are climbing the corporate ladder to never say something that could be construed as an absolute. Academics too tend to shy away from strong exposition. An analyst has to shed that way of communicating. An analyst has opinions on everything in his or her field.

2. Get in the habit of asking yourself, "So what?" whenever you write. You will be surprised at how this evokes a response that turns into actionable advice. Other questions you can ask yourself: "What does this mean for customers of this technology? What does this mean for policy makers

and governments? What does this mean for competitors? What about the employees of the company in question?"
3. An analyst never utters the phrases "time will tell" or "wait and see." You can always tell the non-analyst when he ends a column or blog post with these verbal shrugs that excuse him from taking a stance.
4. Don't trash vendors, especially new ones. If you are going to bring out the big guns and trash a vendor, save it for the big players. The small vendors are the agents of change. They are investing in changing the landscape. Learn from them. Support what they are trying to do when you believe in them. Just don't say anything (publicly) if you don't. Keep in mind, that if you do come down hard on a big vendor by criticizing their core product, or a major strategic direction, you may never do business with them again. They can be vindictive, although their typical response is to cut you off from all communication. The exception is if you are an analyst at a big firm. They may try to get you fired, but will eventually come back and talk to you.
5. Demonstrate authority through insights. As you write show your expertise. Draw comparisons. Retell history. Link to data sources. Pull in supporting opinions from books, academic papers, and other experts. Connect the dots in ways that have not been done before.
6. Be a contrarian. Look for chinks in the accepted wisdom of the day. Is there a high-flying stock on Wall Street? Dig into what could bring it down. Is the reseller channel flocking to a new vendor? Look into the incentives they are getting to do so. Is the Gartner analyst saying one thing? Say the opposite, if you are convinced they are wrong.

With these points in mind, you are ready to start building the basis of your career as an industry analyst.

Working in the same field for five years may qualify you as an expert. The trouble is, if you have been a system administrator or a tool and die worker for five years, you are an expert at what you do but there is little call for industry analysts in those fields. If, on the other hand, you have graduated from system admin to system architecture or if you have been a sales person in the tool and die industry, you may be in a position to be an industry analyst. You should know all the technology, all the products, and something about how the industry works. This book, like the predominant analyst firms, is focused on information technology, but there is a place for acknowledged experts in any industry that is larger than a billion dollars in global revenue. Pharmaceuticals, government contracting, industrial products, entertainment, resource extraction, maritime transport, and airlines are all huge industries where billions are spent. Buyers and sellers need your expertise. If you don't have the requisite 10,000 hours, do not despair. Think about how you can get them. Taking a job in the field is the fastest way, since you will be racking up hours at 2,000+ a year. If you have to hold down a full time job in another area while you spend time on your desired field, it will take much longer. Even at 20 hours a week of research, blogging, or posting podcasts about your selected field means ten years of effort.

Here is a path to becoming an acknowledged expert even before you strike off on your own as an independent analyst. Many of these tasks are going to carry over into your analyst position, so the sooner you start the better.

Create a website

Create an informative website on your space. Populate it continuously with relevant material. You have lots of choices for content management platforms. I have used Drupal, Joomla, even WIX. WordPress is fast becoming the standard platform. You can do everything you need to do with WordPress, it is just not completely intuitive. Keep in mind that when you launch your industry analyst business, this website is still going to be your main site. The domain should still work with the eventual name of your firm, so think ahead! After Gartner I created ThreatChaos.com to write about spyware and cyber crime. When I launched IT-Harvest to cover the IT security space, there was not much in common with the blog name. That issue has hounded me ever since.

Security is extremely important. Often your website will be attacked within 24 hours of being launched. It could be defaced. A spammer may decide to use your domain and email to broadcast their messages. If you say something to upset hackers they could target you for a Denial of Service (DoS) attack. Take some basic precautions. Don't enable the username "admin." Use a strong password. Install Wordfence and lock out accounts after two or three failed attempts.

Your website should look professional and authoritative. Pick a template for your chosen content management system (CMS), be it Drupal, Joomla, or WordPress. Start compiling lists of vendors in your space and break them down into categories. Have separate pages for each category and information about each vendor in each category. The vendors may even see that you have done this. All of a sudden you are on their radar! Having lots of content also creates SEO (search engine optimization). People searching for information in your space should be able to quickly and easily find your website. If you have informative articles about technologies, news, and products other websites will start to link to yours. This will increase your page rank and hopefully put your site on the first page of results for Google searches on keywords. Identify those key words and use them in your posts and titles.

Update your site with new articles every week. Perhaps write about each major product in your field and spread the posts out over a year or two. Go back and update them every month or so.

Use widgets on the front page of your site to display your most recent tweets. Have links to your Twitter handle, LinkedIn profile, and your Facebook page.

Should you host Google ads on your website? I have tried it and cannot recommend it. It does not generate much revenue at all and could very well detract from your perceived objectivity. You could have just written a post about a vendor in your space and ads for their product will appear. Not good.

Your blog

Your blog is the most important feature of your website. You should strive to post at least five times a week. That is every working day. If you can post on the weekends, that is even better. Your posts should be at least 400 words, preferably 600-800. They should each make a point. And the topic, of course, should relate to your industry. Coming up with that many posts is a challenge. Here are some tips for coming up with topics:

- Track news about your industry. Set up Google alerts for the major companies in your industry and their founders/CEOs. You will get a constant stream of alerts in your inbox. Look at each one and ask: How does this news affect the industry? What is interesting, new, different? How does this support a theme I have been writing about?
- Have some central themes you are developing. Create a series of posts for each theme. Spread the posts over several weeks. Pick a day for your major post of the week. Thursday at 11:00 a.m. in your time zone is often identified as the best time to get the most readers.
- Throughout your week keep a running list of topics and ideas to write about. Jot down new ideas as soon as you get out of the shower in the morning, or right before going to bed. Shoot for having more ideas than time to write about them.
- You may begin to get questions from readers. Use these to write more blog posts.
- Use your blog to hone your writing skills and develop your "voice." It should probably be conversational and easy going. But interjecting the "voice of authority" early is a good idea.

A word about detractors: I have found that creating controversy by calling out other bloggers is a waste of time. You will know when you are starting to have an impact when other bloggers start beating *you* up. That is a good thing. The best response is to continue what you are doing, stick to your guns, but do not give your detractors the exposure they seek by responding directly.

Which brings up comments. If you allow comments on your blog, you are going to have two problems. Comment spam will always get through the tools you use to filter it out, so you will be spending time deleting bizarre posts from IP addresses in Russia and trying to blacklist those IP addresses. You will also be spending a lot of time responding to vitriol and very negative sentiments. These can be very depressing to wade through and they can cause writer's block the next time you go to write on a topic. I suggest turning comments off altogether. Besides, today most reactions will show up on your Twitter and Facebook pages.

After a year of posting most days you will have written 130,000 words. That is enough to fill a book! It was only after calculating that I had written 300,000 words for ThreatChaos that it occurred to me that writing a whole book may not be that hard to accomplish. In addition to having established your expertise in your industry, creating all that content will have improved your writing skills dramatically.

Your newsletter

Create a weekly industry insider newsletter and allow people to sign up directly from your website. Economize on how much content you send out. You already have lots of content from your blog and the items you are adding to your website every week. Summarize the blog topics and link back to each blog post. Archive the newsletter on your website. More content! Tip: create a unique title related to the included content for every email blast. If the subject your subscribers see is "Richard's Weekly Newsletter," they are not induced to open it.

Your social media presence

Create a new Twitter account just for your industry interest. If you can get the same Twitter handle as the domain name for your website, great. Take advantage of the ability to dress up your Twitter page. Create a background image that looks like your website. Use your picture as your avatar. Use one that evokes professionalism. No skydiving shots.

Now you are all set, but there is just one problem. There are four little numbers that appear on your page: the number of times you have tweeted, the number of people you follow, the number of people who follow you, and the number of lists you appear on. You must grow all of those stats as quickly as possible. You need to build your Twitter following. The rest of the numbers will take care of themselves. As of this writing, my @cyberwar account has tweeted 12,700 times and has 65,400 followers. My original Twitter handle, @stiennon, has 46,500 followers. I started using Twitter in 2008. You want to get to at least 20,000 followers within a year. Anyone with that many followers *must* be influential, right? Here is how to do it:

The secret to getting followers

The number of followers you have is loosely associated with your influence. The most-followed people are celebrities, journalists, and the early social media experts. When they tweet something, people pay attention. It's the Oprah effect. If Justin Bieber tweets that he likes Coke more than Pepsi, buy stock in Coke and sell Pepsi short. The rest of us are not that popular. The typical industry analyst will have one or two thousand followers; you are going to quickly exceed those numbers.

The goal is to get as many followers as possible as quickly as you can.

Follow followers

You do not want to follow Justin Bieber, CNN Breaking News, or any of the other interesting accounts. You can, but those accounts will not follow you back. You can look at any Twitter account to see the ratio of followed to followers. It is apparent who follows back and who does not. If they have 10,000 followers and only follow 134 people they will not follow you back unless they know you.

Let's get started. You are going to find and follow people who follow back. Go to www.twitter.com/stiennon and follow me. I will follow you back. There's one. Now click on my followers and follow the first twenty that are listed. Don't follow the people I follow, you don't know that they follow back. But the people who follow me have already self-identified as followers. And you only follow the first twenty because they have been recently active. I get about 20 new followers a day organically. Someone who followed me six months ago might not even use Twitter anymore.

Now go to the Twitter page of someone you just followed and click on the list of *their* followers. Follow the first twenty in that list. Rinse and repeat.

If you follow people randomly, you get about 10% follow backs. If you use the technique above it is closer to 50%. Here is how you get that number closer to 90%.

There is a search bar on your Twitter page. Search on "#followback" or "#Teamfollowback." You will get a list of people engaged in building their Twitter follower numbers. Ninety percent of them will follow back.

Now you have to take protective measures to ensure that people who followed you do not think you are a loser who does not follow back. Just look at your list of followers and follow all of them. It's only polite, and you spent about three seconds getting every follower, you don't want to throw that away. You can use an auto-followback tool to take care of this task.

As you will see, this process does not really advance your cause. Once you get over 2,000 followers you can start to cultivate real people that are of interest to you. Follow every journalist, analyst, and blogger in your space. Also follow PR people and the people they follow.

Now to work. Every day of the year you are going to continue getting new followers, but you are also going to start to engage the community.

It is important to realize that most people do not actually read their Twitter stream, that constant flow of tweets from people they follow. They can't. After posting a link to their latest blog post, or a news item that piqued their interest, they then check the "Notifications" button. This will show all of the tweets that are either directed at them, a response to something they tweeted usually, or anyone at all on Twitter that mentioned them—even people they do not follow. In this way they can engage in conversations publicly or respond to comments made about them. Many people will also search on their name, which could be different from their Twitter ID.

This is how you get noticed by the analysts, journalists, and bloggers, even if they do not follow you. You can @ anyone who does not block you. So proceed to:

- Retweet influencers. Don't go crazy, but once a week, at least, retweet something interesting or appropriate they say. If they tweet a link to their latest blog or article or upcoming webinar, retweet that. Help them out. Drive traffic and followers their way. They will notice eventually.
- Mention them. If someone in your industry is mentioned in the press, wins an award, or takes on a new role, tweet that. Either use their name or @ them.
- If you meet someone in your industry, tweet about that.
- Pay particular attention to journalists.
- #FF the vendors and people in your industry. #FF is the hashtag for Follow Friday. I have no idea who invented this, but it has become a Twitter tradition every Friday to tweet lists of great people to follow,

preceded by #FF. Your tweet might be: "#FF Great sources for info on XX @CEO1, @CEO2."

Every time you blog, tweet a link to it. Every time you are quoted anywhere, tweet a link to it. Every YouTube video you put up, tweet it.

As you scour the news and the web for interesting things to write about, you will uncover lots of worthy material. Tweet about it. Your Twitter account will become a valuable information source for anyone tracking your space.

Twitter Lists

Twitter Lists are a great tool of influence. Create a List for your topic, maybe call it Industry Influencers. Then add the folks who qualify to that List. Then you can open a tab on your List. It is surprising how on-topic most people stay, although during a crisis or election season they may drift off subject. Like and re-tweet what these people do. Add comments when you can.

Facebook

Facebook is much harder to leverage, but it is another valuable channel. For now create a Facebook page for your business and populate it with updates and links the way you do on Twitter.

Writing for other publications

As you gain confidence writing, start to look for opportunities to write guest columns for industry publications. Trade magazines (mostly websites now) are always looking for content. You may even land a regular column. There was a time when trade magazines paid for these columns, but in my experience, those days ended in 2008 with the global financial crisis.

Speaking at conferences

If you are not already doing so, start to submit speaking topics to conferences. The more you can get in front of audiences, the better. If your budget or full time job does not allow you to travel, reach out to local chapters of professional societies in your space. Conferences that record pitches and post them are the best. When your presentation is posted, drive as much traffic as you can to it.

Join GLG

Ready to make some money from your expertise? Here is how. Go to www.glg.it and sign up. The Gerson Lehrman Group was formed after the Enron debacle and the fallout that the major investment banks suffered because their own research services were pushing stocks they were underwriting. Wall Street research has been broken away from the big stock traders. This created an opportunity for a new business model. Firms like GLG recruit hundreds of industry experts to answer client questions about those industries. Their clients post inquiries and the experts post their profiles. I have tried half a dozen of these new communities and have found that GLG generates the most revenue. The requirements are very stringent on objectivity. If you work for a publicly traded company you are probably disqualified. Your current employer may consider this moonlighting and forbid you to participate.

The customers of these services are private equity companies, venture capitalists, Wall Street traders, and sometimes the big consulting firms. When they get a project that involves companies in your space, they post an inquiry stating the questions they have. You can browse or search those inquiries and accept them. If the client thinks you are a good match, they will schedule a 30-60 minute call with you.

The calls are great. The clients are usually very smart, young, financial types. But they know next to nothing about your space. You will find that you are getting paid over and over again to deliver the same spiel on your industry. The trends, the market drivers, the best companies, the worst, etc. This is great practice for being an industry analyst. And the money? You set the fee. I charge $500/hr. You may want to start out at $200/hr and then bump it up when you go out on your own. The very best thing about this revenue stream is that the payment process is so smooth. After the call you visit the website, enter the number of minutes you spent on the call and in ten days the money is deposited in your bank account. When IT-Harvest was getting off the ground there were many months when GLG meant the difference between a late and an on-time mortgage payment.

Your book

Yes, you have to write a book. There is no more direct path to becoming an acknowledged expert than to become a published author on your industry. A book will get you speaking engagements. Your bio will lead off with "author of." You may even make money from book sales. And the best time to write your book is before you hang up your shingle as an independent analyst. In the next chapter, I will share all I have learned about writing and publishing books.

How to Write and Publish a Book

There are many successful analysts who have not written a book. Part of the reason is that they are too busy to take the time. That is why the best time to write a book is while you are still employed in industry but before you join an analyst firm or strike out on your own. Admittedly, you will have time during the first two years of being on your own because you will not be at full capacity. But when you are struggling to pay bills it is hard to call up the type of motivation it takes to plug away at writing a book.

So, the best time to tackle a book is during your ramp up to becoming an analyst. After the long list of tasks laid out in the previous chapter needed to build your expertise, it may seem like piling a book project on top of everything else is just too much. But the book can help. If you are immersed in writing something relevant to your industry, there will be many topics that can be dual-purposed. Post the first draft of your thoughts on each chapter of your book to your blog. Make sure you add a footnote that states: "Excerpted from the yet-to-be-published book…" Now your work is triple purposed. You are populating your blog and website with great content, you are writing your book, and you are simultaneously beginning the marketing of your book.

If you are like me, writing a book may never have occurred to you. It is a big time commitment and takes focus over at least a year. I am someone who did not pursue a Master's degree after college because I was afraid of the requirement of writing a thesis. I am a terrible procrastinator and hate doing assigned tasks. (That all changed when "assigned tasks" turned into customer demands. I am very motivated to finish customer projects on time.) As an engineer, writing was never on my list of enjoyable tasks. But while at Webroot Software, I started one of the first blogs on security, threatchaos.com, and discovered I like to write. Now, writing is my favorite occupation after public speaking. When I launched

IT-Harvest, I found myself presenting at a conference in Halifax, Nova Scotia. A documentary producer who was working on a special report on cybercrime asked me if I would sit for a few minutes and be interviewed for his piece. His crew shot me for an hour. When we were done he said, "Wow, you really know this topic, have you written a book?" That was when it first occurred to me that maybe I should.

In the summer of 2008 Russia invaded South Ossetia, part of Georgia. At the same time they launched attacks against government websites and attempted to swamp servers with packets. This first instance of cyberwar (by some definitions) spawned four books on cyberwar. One of them was mine. After writing *Surviving Cyberwar* I realized that writing a Master's thesis was not such a daunting task. I went back to school, wrote that thesis, and turned it into another book (*There Will Be Cyberwar*). Along the way I learned something else: there is nothing as professionally satisfying as completing a manuscript and shipping it off to be published. You are compelled to start writing the next book.

Picking a topic

Writing just any book is not good enough. The subject matter has to be relevant to your analyst business. It has to build your reputation as an expert on the topic. So think about and research topics and titles. I have found that there are very few books written from an industry analyst's perspective on their own industry. Perhaps a book titled "Getting to know the X industry" would be a good place to start. The advantage to writing on your industry is that your target audience is also your addressable market for the analyst work you will be performing.

Pick a style. There are a few styles you should consider before you start to write. I find the easiest book to write is what I call the 'extended blog.' That is pretty much the voice I use for this book and I used it successfully in *UP and to the RIGHT: Strategy and Tactics of Analyst Influence*. I certainly have received much more positive feedback on this style than my first book, *Surviving Cyberwar*, which was published and marketed as a textbook even though it was written to be a *New York Times* bestseller. Not everything works out as planned.

Another style is called narrative nonfiction. This is the bestseller style you may be familiar with from Tom Peters or George Gilder or Malcolm Gladwell. Their books are laced with stories of real world people that illustrate their overall theme. Storytelling is the most powerful form of human communication and these masters make good use of it.

You could also adopt the style of an extended industry report. While this would be a valuable project, it entails a lot more work, a lot more research, and is probably a longer work.

Rather than an industry review, you may want to expand on some insight you have had on what drives the industry. Possible titles could be "Winners and Losers in the X Industry," or "Why the X Industry is Poised to Change Everything," or "The Next Big Thing in X." You get the idea.

You could pick ten leaders in your industry and write their stories. Or you could write about ten failures in your industry. All would be great books that would be well received.

One word of warning. A technical book is probably not a good idea for helping you along your way to becoming an industry analyst. A technical book could ignite a career as a CTO or a consultant, but it does not demonstrate the industry insights that you want to promulgate.

The goal is to have written "The Book" on your industry, one that everyone else has to cite when they write about the industry and one that has to be on the book shelf or e-reader of everyone in the business.

Start with an outline

Are you familiar with agile programming? I have found that agile techniques are perfect for creating long manuscripts such as books. If you are a member of that species often referred to as "engineers," you will find that you are very comfortable with this approach.

Start with an outline. First, just jot down every single topic that should be included. Get 20 or 30 or more on your computer. Then break each topic down into ten or so subtopics. Arrange them in a logical order. There is your outline. Don't write the introduction and the last chapter until you are done writing the first draft.

Set your goal for page length. Shoot for 200 pages. That's 50,000 words. Take your 100 or so sub topics and write 500 words on each one (on average). Voila, you have just written a book.

Every book needs a story arc. The first chapter has to pull the reader in and each chapter has to lead to the next. Put the big message, the climax (the aha! moment), in the middle. Tail off by building on that climax; lessons learned, what this all means, etc. Put supporting and reference material in the appendices.

On writing

If you are blogging regularly you are probably pretty comfortable with putting words together into sentences, sentences into paragraphs, paragraphs into chapters. But what about finding the time and place to write? Once you are comfortable with the fact that you are a writer, you are probably putting that "thirst for knowledge" that every analyst has to work. You are already researching the writing process. Read the many writing blogs and look at the resources in Appendix I. Watch the talks and interviews that authors have given on YouTube. You will become fascinated with how other writers write. I once shared a limo with George Gilder and took the opportunity to ask him how he managed to be so productive and his answer was that he wrote every day from 5:00 to 7:00 a.m. Neal Stephenson rises early and edits the ten pages he wrote the day before. After loading his current progress into memory, he is able to scratch out the next ten pages. He claims to stop around 2:00 p.m. every day. Of course this reflects the immortal advice from Hemingway: write every day and stop when you know what you are going to write the next day. In this way you overcome the delay and possibly the procrastination that comes from staring at a blank page/screen.

If you can carve out a schedule that allows you to write every day, you are better than I am. I need large blocks of time to write, a minimum of four hours. And my brain, fingers, and eyes do not even work together until after 10:00 a.m. I retreat to my writing shed or the public library and write for several weeks, hopping around, writing the easy parts, outlining the hard parts. Then I schedule a week in a hotel with a view of Lake Huron for a major sprint. I can usually write 25,000 words in such a retreat. Part of the reason it works so well is that I have carved out this time to write; I have a target, and I am paying for the luxury of time alone. This pressure makes it easier to shut off Facebook for the duration. I wrote *UP and to the RIGHT* in five days at a hilltop bed and breakfast near Nashville, Tennessee, called Butterfly Meadows.

There is a tool you have to use for your writing. I discovered it the day before starting *UP and to the RIGHT*. I had been dreaming of a word processor that made it easier to write in the chunks that the agile process calls for. I also wanted something that would show a progress bar against a target number of words as I wrote. When I finish a great sprint and am a thousand words short of my goal for the day, it helps to see that progress bar turning from yellow to green but not quite there yet. I pick another two topics and get 500 words each written and then I can quit for dinner.

The best tool I have found for writing is called Scrivener. It was created by a programmer in England and is experiencing tremendous success as more and more authors and students discover how powerful it is for long manuscripts.

I learned how to use Scrivener in a couple of hours of watching YouTube videos. It is available for Mac and PC and only costs $45 (get Scrivener at www.literatureandlatte.com).

The left hand side shows all the chapters, the appendices, and the front matter (title page, copyright page, dedication). The biggest advantage of

Scrivener over Microsoft Word is that chapter organization is so easy. Most books created with Word end up being separate files for each chapter. When you decide to add a chapter or move chapters around (and you will), you have to rename all the files! In Scrivener you just drag the folders up or down and insert new material anywhere. You can also assign word targets to each chapter and there is a project status bar that tracks progress towards your total. There is also a daily target that is reset every night at midnight.

The other amazing capability—really a new paradigm—is the compile function. You hit the compile button and are presented with powerful features to completely control the final output form of your book. I will use the compile function a hundred times to get the final product. If you have ever written a computer program you will recognize this paradigm. Compile-test-fix-compile until it is just right. For publishing through Print on Demand sources such as Amazon's Kindle Direct Publishing (KDP) you need to upload a PDF of the inside material of your book. I have used this successfully for eight different projects (see ITH-Press.com for the complete catalog). For this book, I have decided to transition to Adobe InDesign for the final layout and production of the PDF. A professional tool such as InDesign gives you much more control over the final look and feel of the book and makes image placement much easier. Adding small graphic and typological details is also easier. I hired a book designer to do this. Reedsy is a great place to find both editors and designers.

There are other useful features to Scrivener. The corkboard view mimics the way a lot of authors organize their thoughts into notecards. Another feature is you can hit the "Compose" button and get rid of all the control panels and just see a blank "sheet of paper" so you can write without distraction. Use Scrivener. You can thank me later.

One final tool that can help: get yourself an AlphaSmart. This is a clunky plastic keyboard that is just meant for writing a lot of words. It has a four-line LCD screen so you can see what you are writing and it runs on rechargeable batteries. You can get 800 hours on a charge, far surpassing the time a laptop provides for writing. The AlphaSmart is for power sprints. Step away from your computer. Find a good place to settle in and get all your thoughts down into words. Don't worry about spelling or punctuation. Just get your words out of your brain and into the AlphaSmart. When you get back to your computer, plug it in via USB cable, open any empty text document and hit "send." Then take a break as the AlphaSmart *re-types* your words into the document. Because it is using the standard keyboard protocol to talk to your computer there is no need for any software. It will work with any computer that has a keyboard. Cut and paste the new text into Scrivener and clean it up.

The AlphaSmart seems expensive at $600. I buy them for $25 on eBay. Much of this book was written on my AlphaSmart.

Now send your draft to your editor. Yes, you need an editor. This is someone who has studied writing and understands the art and science of authorship, be it fiction or nonfiction. He or she will help ensure that your book is readable, transitions from chapter to chapter, and just makes sense. Your editor may be the only person who reads your book cover to cover before it is published.

You may also want to employ a copy editor for catching all those misplaced commas and dangling participles. Also, get someone in your industry to read it with an eye towards fact checking. Save yourself the embarrassment I suffered from getting the address of the National Security Agency wrong in *Surviving Cyberwar*. A knowledgeable industry person will catch the glaring errors and perhaps give you great feedback on how to improve the book. You will find people are very interested in your project and happy to participate in its success. Early readers may even provide the blurbs for the back cover and write an Amazon review for you.

Publishing

Anyone who has been through the traditional publishing process has horror stories to tell about inept editors, clueless marketing, stupid pricing, and drawn-out lead times. But despite all of that, for the purposes of becoming an acknowledged expert it is still best to get published in the traditional manner. There is an onus attached to the self-published author that has to be overcome with great writing, content, and marketing. As far as your author reputation is concerned, you are done once you publish traditionally. The quality and impact of your book are secondary.

Picking a publisher. When you write fiction you have to submit a completed manuscript to dozens of publishers and often enlist an agent to help you. It is a grueling process and the history of publishing is rife with stories of great authors who were rejected repeatedly.

Non-fiction authors have a much easier path. Most nonfiction publishers will accept submissions of proposals instead of completed manuscripts. Even though I am going to argue for self-publishing further down, I still recommend going through the proposal submission process with a couple of publishers. It is educational and will help hone your plan for the book. Find the publishers that have published books like yours. Browse a book store if you can find one. Amazon has complete publisher information for every book they sell and most publishers have submission instructions on their websites. You can even find their acquisition editors on LinkedIn. Send him or her a brief description about why the world will end if your book is not published and see if they have any interest. Just complying with the long submission forms and cumbersome process of identifying your target audience, the size of that audience, and the competing books already out there is a valuable exercise. One of the publishers may even offer you a contract.

I learned a lot about the publishing industry in writing my first book, *Surviving Cyberwar*.

The time was ripe, just after the cyber attacks on the country of Georgia. There were no modern books on the topic. I knew the topic, and I had the credentials (former Gartner analyst!). But I was already busy launching (actually re-launching) IT-Harvest and could not justify the time, including a field trip to Estonia, to interview people on the front. So I tried a new route. I approached several magazines about serializing the book. I offered to post a monthly column "from the front lines" and the magazine would pay me $1,500/column. Sadly, this was the fall of 2008 just as the global financial crisis was materializing and all the trade press, even the ones I had written for regularly in the past, had a new policy: no paid freelancers. But nine months in to this frustration I was contacted by one of the editors I had first approached. He had just taken a job as an acquisition editor for an imprint of one of the largest book publishers in the world. I was in. They even signed me up for three titles.

But I still had the financial issue. So my sales guy (yes, I have a salesperson. You will too. See the chapter on the analyst business) had a brilliant idea. Get a vendor to sponsor the writing of the book. Here is how it works: the vendor pays a lump sum ($80,000 in this case) and for that they get:

- The forward written by one of their subject matter experts.
- I speak at three of their events.
- Every time I speak about the book I flash a slide from my sponsor.
- They get a 25% discount on bulk orders of the book. The publisher will even print a special cover with their branding. So keep this idea in mind. It only works when you are already an industry analyst and you can assign a dollar value to your speaking engagements.

Unfortunately, my publisher sold text books. So, my "*New York Times* bestseller" was sold to universities at the ridiculous price of $39 for a soft cover. To date it has sold 3,500 copies, which is more that Carl von Clausewitz's *On War* sold in its first three years, but is nowhere close to my expectations. My one dollar per book royalty is pretty typical of the industry. But the important thing is becoming a **published author**. As soon as you are published you acquire a second name—Author of—which appears in newspaper quotes and your bio at all the conferences to which you get invited to speak. The speaking fees alone more than justify the work you put into the book. On top of that, helping establish you as an analyst is of immeasurable value.

Oh, and all the wonderful marketing ability that traditional publishers are supposed to have? It does not exist. I had to arrange and pay for my own book launch event. I had to purchase the books to sign! It cost $500 to launch at the National Press Club in DC. Imagine my surprise when my editor showed up with his boss to get free coffee and doughnuts and a signed copy of my book. (Always have food at your book launch, otherwise the journalists won't show up.)

Publishing Services

The advent of Print on Demand coupled with the centralized marketplace of Amazon has given rise to hundreds of "small presses." They typically charge a range of fees for editing, artwork, and formatting. They can publish under their imprint or you can publish yourself. Check out ITH-Press.com to see the formula I came up with.

Self-publishing

If you cannot convince any traditional publisher of impeding Armageddon because they won't publish your book, the next alternative is the self-publishing route. Self-publishing has three advantages over traditional publishing: time, money, and marketing.

Time

After your manuscript is complete you are looking at at least six months, usually a year, to publish with a traditional publisher. It is possible to self-publish in three months. I am working on a process to get that down to three weeks. If you write a time-sensitive book, this can make a tremendous difference to sales. You don't want your book reflecting ancient history in your industry when it becomes available. This change in publishing times may even be disruptive. While online versions of newspapers and magazines have displaced print, in part because of the immediacy of the web, books are still always out of date when they are published. If you bought this book soon after it became available, you can know that I probably put it to bed just four weeks ago. Think about it, you could write a summary of major events that occurred in your industry derived from the blog posts you are writing already. You could publish a book every January summarizing the previous year's events and your analysis of them. You could even even do that every six months.

Money

Profits from each book are ten times higher if you self-publish. Book writing can actually be lucrative. You also get your royalties every month instead of the arcane twice yearly, six months in arrears, which traditional publishing follows. That's right. If your book is launched in May, you will not see the first penny until the following January–and that will only cover books sold through June. There is a big difference in incentive to market your book. If you do a series of book signings and sell an extra hundred books, you do not reap the benefit for half a year. You are flying blind. You do not even know how sales are going other than the occasional review or comment from someone you meet at a conference. Self-publishing allows you to check on sales every day, or multiple times during the day. You can test the impact on sales of an email blast. You can see if sales increase when you write a column for an online magazine or you are quoted in the *Wall Street Journal*. When I published *There Will Be Cyberwar*, my friend who happens to own TheCoolTV had me create a 15 second ad for the book. Within a couple of days my ad was running on a music video TV channel that apparently has millions of viewers. I could watch sales throughout the day. Total sales from the TV ad? As near as I can tell: zero. Chalk it up to an inexpensive experiment in marketing. Viewers of music video channels are probably not interested in arcane topics like cyberwar and revolutions in military affairs.

Marketing

As you research the book industry you will notice the advice to have a "platform" for your book. This is industry jargon for a website, Twitter account with lots of followers, a YouTube Channel, Facebook page, and a blog. You already have that, of course. Here is how you can begin to market your book:
- Update your Twitter background with your book cover design.
- Announce availability on your website. Link directly to the Amazon listing of your book.
- Tweet that the book is available. Tweet a lot. Your followers will forgive you for the blatant marketing. You just wrote a book. You are allowed to beat your chest.
- Update your LinkedIn title to Author of …
- Blast your contacts with an announcement. Even your non-industry contacts will not be offended. This is a big life event that they should know about. Do this on a day when you have lots of time to respond

to emails. When I announced the launch of *UP and to the RIGHT* to my 3,200 contacts, I received 300 positive responses over the next 24 hours. Now that I have over 13,000 connections on LinkedIn I truly have a valuable platform.
- Send a special announcement to everyone on your newsletter mailing list.
- Issue a press release.
- Send copies to people who review books.
- Write columns on the book topic for trade press.
- Reach out to radio talk shows. They often do author interviews. If you have not done a lot of radio, be warned that it can be frustrating. You can barely get a cogent thought out before there is another commercial break. Just go with it and relax. Make note of all the podcasts in your topic area. Reach out to them. In the meantime your tweeting and posting to LinkedIn about your radio appearances and podcast interviews builds the perception that your book is gaining a lot of attention. Sales will trickle in.

Print on Demand

The biggest revolution to hit book publishing has been Print on Demand (POD). There are several companies that do this. I use KDP, Amazon's POD service (kdp.amazon.com). You are going to upload your book in PDF format to KDP. You used Scrivener to compile in PDF format or your designer has created it. On top of the book itself you need a book cover in PDF format. Hire a professional designer for that. Low cost options, about $250, are possible with someone from fiverr.com. After you upload your manuscript, KDP will give you the exact dimensions of your cover including the size of the spine, which varies based on number of pages. Give those dimensions to your graphic artist and upload the finished cover when it is ready. Then you set your price and give the okay to publish. Within three days, your book is online on Amazon. As soon as you publish, KDP provides you with cover and internal files that are transferred over to a Kindle ebook version. Go through that process as soon as possible, otherwise your Facebook page and Twitter stream will be filled with people asking when the digital version will be available. It takes Amazon several days to notice that the two formats should be linked. It helps to contact customer support at Amazon and ask them to make the linkage. That way someone who finds your book will be presented with both formats.

Amazon may be responsible for the demise of Borders Books and the other book stores that used to line Main Street, but it has also made the self-publishing industry possible. It is especially good for nonfiction. Fiction authors have a much harder time marketing than do nonfiction authors. Nonfiction books are different. Your industry key words are probably in your title or subtitle. You have probably already done this search when you researched your topic. In the future, anyone who searches on your industry is going to find your book. If your sales are going well, your book will be the first result.

Well, that is not quite accurate. Amazon search is hackable, ludicrously so. Here, for the first time in print, are the instructions for hacking Amazon search. This could be fixed overnight by Amazon, and I expect it to be fixed every time I do it. But it works today.

Search Amazon for "analyst influence." Well, look at that, UP and to the RIGHT is the first result! How can that be? Eight years after publication the book sells at most one a week. How is that done? Simple. I search on "analyst influence" every so often and I click through to my book. That is how Amazon judges what gets moved to the top of search results: click-throughs.

After you click through to your book, look at the URL that got you there. It looks like this:

https://www.amazon.com/UP-RIGHT-Strategy-Tactics- Influence-ebook/dp/B008I5O154/ref=sr_1_1?dchild=1&keywords=analyst+influence

See that? The search terms are in the URL. Now when you post a link to your book, use this URL. Put it in your LinkedIn profile, your Twitter page, etc. Each time anybody clicks on the link it tells the Amazon algorithm that they found your book through search and it enhances your book's position in the results page.

Here is why KDP is the best option for Print on Demand. Amazon lists KDP titles as "in-stock" even though they may not actually have any in their warehouses. Other POD suppliers may get the "ships in three days" note under the title, or even Out of Stock. When a customer purchases your book, Amazon prints it and ships it the same day. You can still smell the ink when you get it the next day. KDP also allows you to purchase your own book at cost so you can order "author copies" in bulk for your book signings. I have purchased thousands this way.

It used to be possible to game Amazon a bit. If you purchased your own book from them, it counted towards Amazon's overall ranking. If you actually purchased 1,000 books a day for a week you would probably make it to #1 on Amazon. I suspect that some authors have done that. Obviously it is expensive and you would have to be pretty brazen to attempt it. Besides, Amazon finally caught on and does not appear to give bulk orders the same credence as purchases from multiple readers. I recommend sending review copies to fifty or so people in your industry, potential customers, journalists, and your vendor clients. Any friends or contacts that offer to write an Amazon review should get a copy, too. If you are not already an Amazon Prime subscriber, sign up so that you get free shipping (within the United States). For every book you buy at list price you earn your royalty, so the expense is not as bad as you might first expect.

Amazon has the ability to discount your book price. This is great because the discount is taken out of Amazon's cut, so you benefit from the lower selling price while keeping the same profit. There is also another trick of the trade that Aaron Shepard, author of *POD For Profit*, describes. Amazon strives to be the low-cost seller of all books. If you publish through another source, in particular IngramSpark, which is part of the giant book distributor Ingram, your book will also be listed on Barnes and Noble's website. Set your pricing lower on that site. Amazon will pick up on that and discount your book on their site to match or beat the B&N price. I have never done this because of the disadvantage of having a book listed as "not in stock," or "ships in three days."

Buying ads. You can pay Amazon for placement in search. You can even choose to have your book ad show up on the screen of an idle Kindle. Facebook too is often used to push books. I have found that at the very best you can break even with Amazon marketing service (AMS). Facebook has never worked for my books, although many fiction authors have succeeded in boosting their books on Facebook. You would think LinkedIn would be the perfect place to advertise a nonfiction book, but this is not the case. For some reason, LinkedIn's advertising platform is geared towards branding, not selling. You cannot create an ad that links to your Amazon listing. It has to link to a landing page where you have to attempt to get someone to Buy Now. I have spent several thousand dollars on LinkedIn ads with zero sales. It is much more productive to just post about your book to your timeline, especially if you have lots of followers in your space.

Now that you are a published author, you can start to capitalize on this. Your salesperson can reach out to your vendor clients and your speaking agent can reach out to conferences. Both are leveraging your status of published author. Vendor clients will purchase books in bulk and hire you for book signings in their booth or their hospitality suites at conferences. Conferences will start to pay you speaking fees to keynote events. You may make only $10k from book sales spread over two years, not a game changer. But you will earn hundreds of thousands from speaking engagements and new clients.

Starting Your Own Firm

The transition from acknowledged expert to industry analyst can occur anytime. The biggest question is financial. When can you afford to quit your day job and launch your new firm? In an ideal world, you will have six months' to a year's worth of living expenses saved up. In the real world, you may find yourself on the street without a job and no savings with little notice. Either way, the best path is to quit your job, announce your new role as an industry analyst, and get your first paying client on the same day. Of all the companies I have started, the ones that have succeeded have sold something before launching. As a prolific blogger, the maintainer of an important information resource on your industry, and the author of a book, you may have been turning down paid speaking engagements, or strategic consulting gigs, already. When you accept one of those opportunities is the time to launch.

Here is how the independent analyst business works.

End user clients versus vendors

There are three types of clients for an industry analyst: the end users of the types of products sold in your industry, vendors in your space, and investment firms.

End user organizations, be they banks, manufacturers, government agencies, or hospitals, are looking for expert guidance in product selection, contract negotiation, deployment, and staffing advice. If you manage to sell to this class of client you have three tremendous advantages. First, there are a lot more end user companies than there are vendors, so you have a larger addressable market. Second, every time you work with a client who is selecting and deploying products in your space, you add to your expertise. By seeing firsthand what multi-million dollar technology investments look like at many organizations, you gain insight and experience that cannot be achieved any other way. And finally, the vendors view you as influential, so they are going to come to you and possibly engage you.

The downside of end user clients is they are not accustomed to paying the exorbitant fees that an industry analyst commands. Even the top partner at a large consulting firm or law firm rarely can bill more than $500/hr. Vendors, on the other hand, have marketing budgets to spend and there is a pretty well-established fee structure for paid speakers and white papers. Most independent analysts serve the vendor space. That is the path I am going to suggest. There are ways to move into the end user space that you can start exploring once you have established your business.

The third category of clients is investors. They are looking for expert guidance to help with their investment decisions. They want to know the potential for growth in various segments of your space and the prospects of particular players. I have already mentioned GLG and will introduce other opportunities later.

Vendors

Vendors of products in your space strive to improve the market acceptance of their products. Their marketing and PR teams have budget to devote to this. Here is how you convince vendors to spend money with you. I call it the influence funnel.

At the wide end of the funnel are all the activities you have been engaging in to become an acknowledged expert: your blogging, tweeting, and book(s). You need to convince the vendors that that expertise is recognized by their target market—that you are influential. So the next stage of the funnel is appearing in media. Your column in a major trade magazine, the quotes that appear in mainstream media, the videos of your presentations at major conferences, and of course the number of followers you have on Twitter all demonstrate your influence. Create a special page on your website that tracks all of your speaking engagements and another page that reposts all of your quotes and appearances on TV and radio programs. Your website is going to transition from a purely informational site to a branding tool for your new firm.

You are going to have to do your own PR to build those quotes in mainstream media. Start collecting the email addresses of any journalist that writes about your space: the people, companies, technologies, and trends. Reach out to them when they publish and offer any insights you may have. Suggest that if they ever need an objective source for quotes to feel free to reach out. Provide your cell phone number. Most industry articles are not complete without a quote from an industry analyst and journalists will go back to the same source over and over. But sometimes they are on deadline and their usual source is on an airplane. If they have your number, you may get a call.

The one activity that is sure to get you noticed by the vendors is to write about them. If, for instance, you write about a new development in the industry and mention the three or four big players in the space, every other vendor in the space will reach out to you within 48 hours with requests to brief you on what they do. Take those briefings.

Briefings are at the bottom of the funnel. They are how you generate leads and often the beginning of the sales cycle with a vendor.

Objectivity

Before we get to how to sell to vendors, we have to address a critical question. An independent analyst must be objective. You have to walk the fine line between helping a vendor and being a reliable source of non-tainted advice. Newspapers and magazines have been faced with this dilemma ever since they offered advertising. The way they handle it is to separate ad sales from editorial oversight. But you are a one-person show and cannot do that. So you have to abide by some rules:

Never say unsupported things about vendors. While you may recommend vendor solutions to your paying end user clients (when you get those), you never recommend a vendor in print or any other media. You limit yourself to talking about their strengths and weaknesses. Always include those weaknesses.

When you provide quotes for a vendor press release, never mention the vendor in the quote. Your quote is there to support the validity of the space, the problem addressed, or the technology, not the product.

Think hard before accepting a position on a vendor's advisory board, or to sit on the board of directors, even at a startup. From a cold hearted financial perspective it does not make sense. Advisory roles rarely pay. Even board roles at a startup do not pay. The equity for these positions is usually 0.5 to 1.5% vested over three to four years. The final payout could be life changing but the odds are slim of that happening in less than ten years. In the meantime, every competitive vendor is going to avoid working with you because you are conflicted. That said, sometimes it is hard to turn a friend down. As of this writing I am on the advisory boards of Phosphorous, an IoT management company, GroupSense, a threat intelligence service, and on the board of Anitian, a security and compliance automation company. See what I did there? When claiming independence I must be transparent about any conflicts I may have.

You cannot own stock or shares in any publicly traded vendor. Those analysts that do must declare their ownership. This will immediately call into question your objectivity. It is much better to avoid those conflicts of interest altogether by divesting your portfolio before you become an analyst. This goes for immediate family members, too. This can be a problem if your spouse, children, or parents work for a vendor and have stock plans.

You can never take a "piece of the action." This is the most frequent conflict I am presented with. The proposition always sounds so innocent: If you uncover an opportunity that leads to a sale, the vendor promises to compensate you, usually as much as a 10% finder's fee. You just can't do this. If this means walking away from millions of dollars, you can consider hanging up your analyst hat and becoming a business development person.

There is no oversight of industry analysts' objectivity, but the market will quickly punish anyone who steps over the line. Look at Aberdeen, a once-successful research firm that became known for writing reports that would support anything a vendor was willing to pay for. Aberdeen was eventually sold to Harte Hanks, which attempted to revise its model. In 2006 the *Wall Street Journal* had this to say about Aberdeen:

> There were many excesses during the Internet bubble; one involved the Aberdeen Group, which passed itself off as a technology consulting and research operation, but which was for the most part a "pay-for-praise" operation. If you saw an Aberdeen report saying that Acme MicroMacro sold world-class solutions, you could be sure that Acme had written Aberdeen a world-class check.

Beware the vendor that steps over the line and requests you to do something that would compromise your objectivity. A single infraction could force you out of business.

Briefings

Now that you are armed, it is time to talk about briefings. As you get the word out that you have become an industry analyst you will get a flood of requests, especially when you write and publish about your space. A typical briefing is an hour-long presentation by the vendor usually delivered over GoToMeeting, Webex, or Zoom. Request that the vendor also send over a copy of the slide deck for your records. The briefing is your chance to (1) get to know the people that represent the vendor, and (2) become conversant in the vendor's products. Smaller vendors will often have the CEO make the presentation and their outside PR person will be there to take notes for follow up. With larger vendors, you will be talking to the product team. The vendor's goal is to win you over, get you to support their mission, and even write positively about them. You have one goal: to demonstrate that you "get it," that you understand the product and the value it has to solving the stated problem.

Vendors give lots of briefings. When they talk to the big analyst firms, they often run into the curmudgeon factor. The analyst appears full of himself, unwilling to listen, and only provides feedback of the "you are going to fail" variety. Don't be that analyst. Gartner analysts will even make a point of being close-lipped, often suggesting that only vendor clients get the benefit of their wisdom and that briefings are one-way exchanges of information, vendor to analyst. You, on the other hand, are going to be forthright, even helpful. Interject with questions. Suggest companies that have similar or different approaches. Offer to introduce them to people in the industry that can help them, even potential customers. Demonstrate that you "get" what they are trying to do. Occasionally the vendor briefing will give you an idea to write about. Do that and mention the vendor.

Many analysts are pugnacious with vendors. They approach vendors with suspicion and accuse them of marketing hype and outright lies. But they miss an important point. It's the vendors who created this industry, not the analysts. The vendors recognized a need, researched solutions, built products, took them to market, and acquired customers. The successful vendors listened closely to customers (often many more than the paltry 12,000 customers that Gartner has) and evolved their product in response to customer feedback. A good analyst looks past marketing jargon and inflated sales figures and delves into the product and its features. The products are a reflection of market demand for functionality. When a vendor reaches out to brief you on a new function, pay particular attention. The vendor has researched their client's needs and identified a differentiating capability that they have invested in. During the briefing try to get to the bottom of what drove this innovation. It may turn into an "aha!" moment for you, one that you can be the first to write about, which in turn elevates your status as an analyst who can call the market accurately.

Even when a vendor appears to be on the wrong track, do not be dismissive. Help them out. In the politest terms, state that you have not seen the demand they are talking about, that a different technology has more promise, or suggest that their messaging needs re-working. Even if you are convinced that this product is going to fail, give them some nuggets of your wisdom. They may come back in six months with, "You were right, here is how we have changed direction. Are you available for speaking engagements?" Even when the vendor meets your expectations and they fail, you will be surprised how often you get on the phone with the same marketing people, only now they are working for another vendor.

At the end of a successful briefing, you have demonstrated that you "get it," and you have provided some good intel on the industry. What's next? Do you sell them on your many services? No. Not unless they specifically ask about your services do you go into your sales pitch. As an independent analyst, you are not a salesperson. That is what your salesperson is for.

The Triple Play Business Model

Many of the most successful independent analysts use the same business structure: what I call the Triple Play success formula. You, the analyst, are the product. Your salesperson sells the product, and your bookkeeper sends invoices. You may be a one-person show when you start out, but you are going to need someone to do the sales and someone to do the accounts receivables.

You are going to have to hire an administrator. This person will help with your travel, your briefing schedule, fielding calls from journalists, keeping track of expenses, and most importantly, getting money in the door by annoying clients until they pay.

Sales

You need a salesperson. It is a great advantage to have someone else selling your capabilities. The vendor is used to dealing with salespeople from the large analyst firms. The salesperson does the negotiating, delivers the proposals, and nags the vendor until they agree to engage you. You work behind the scenes writing the proposals, approving the terms, and occasionally asking your salesperson, "What have you done for me lately?"

Here is how we found an amazing sales person. You need someone who understands the analyst business. In other words, they have to have worked for another firm. How do you find such a person? Easy: place an ad on Craigslist for two locations—Stamford, Connecticut, where Gartner is headquartered, and Fort Meyers, Florida, where Gartner's inside sales team is employed. You don't care where the salesperson lives. We did not meet our sales person until he had been working for us for three years.

Compensation

The best way to start out is if your salesperson can work part time for you while holding down a full-time position in a non-conflicting job. You are going to pay your salesperson commission only. Your business has too many ups and downs to justify a salary and benefits. If you are having a few slow months, you want your salesperson to feel it too so they are motivated to bring in more business.

A good salesperson commands more than $200k in income. You cannot provide that until revenue is up to a million dollars.

How much commission? Start with 15% and build in generous increases up to 20-25% of sales over a certain target. Say 15% of the first $100k, 20% of the next, and 25% on anything over $200k in the year.

Your products

Before we discuss the various products/services you provide for a fee as an industry analyst, you have to spend some time considering what your daily rate is. Your daily rate will provide the basis for keeping the pricing for your various products consistent. Keep in mind that the Gartner rate for an analyst for either a speaking engagement or a day-long strategy session is $25k. It may be possible to match that if you are one of the few analysts in a rapidly growing space with lots of demand. But you will probably start lower than that. Do not think about your rates in terms of previous salaries you have had. When vendor clients engage you, they are purchasing your time and paying a significant premium for your brand/reputation. Having you host a webinar or speak at one of their events is bound to draw a wider audience than they could get without an independent analyst. Don't think that $1,000 a day translates into $200k a year. Even while I was one of the most engaged analysts at Gartner, I only did 50 days a year of speaking and strategy sessions. Start with 50 days as your annual capacity. It you need $200k a year then your daily rate is $4,000. If the strain of traveling that much gets too great, charge more.

Here are the products you should be selling

Annual access

Another name for this is a retainer. During the course of twelve months you are available to the vendor for scheduled conference calls, to answer email questions, or even take late night calls from the CEO who is contemplating a change in strategy or looking for your input on hiring a PR firm or a new VP of Sales. The engagement also includes a full-day strategy session to kick off the relationship. One or two customer events or webinars will complete the value proposition. Charge four times your daily rate. And most importantly, insist on getting paid up front for the year. Most finance departments will push back on this, but it is the industry norm as set by the big firms. Occasionally, you may have a giant company that is unbending. Don't go below a quarterly payment plan. You may also have a startup that is as worried about cash flow as you are. Help them out, but once again, do not allow them to negotiate a monthly payment plan. That builds a perception that something is going to happen every month and through no fault of yours, there may be months where the client is not even available for calls or email questions. Collecting from small firms is very cumbersome. You will spend more time getting your monthly installments than you spend on engaging with the product team. Large companies have their own problems, but once you are in their system and have a PO, getting paid is straightforward, although they create friction to stretch out the process. We had one client who moved to a third-party supplier solution. We had to purchase tickets for each invoice submitted, about $25 each. This was just too offensive so we insisted that we mail them invoices. They said fine and gave us an address in Puerto Rico to send invoices to! Payments were made from their Singapore office. You too will learn the joys of being a small business.

Speaking engagements

A speaking engagement could include: presenting an hour-long pitch at a customer prospect dinner or breakfast seminar, presenting at a customer advisory board meeting, or even presenting at a sales offsite. The last are fun. The audience is usually very receptive, and if you attend the evening's entertainment, be protective of your liver. Charge your full day rate plus travel expenses for speaking engagements. Invoice for the event as soon as you have a PO or signed agreement. Insist on payment before you get on a plane. Tell the client early that you cannot guarantee the date they are interested in until you have payment. This is the only chance you have to get paid on time. The person putting the event together is completely focused on making it happen, he or she has budget, and their finance department understands the need to reserve time on your calendar. If you do the event without upfront payment, you will be thrown into the payment-delay cycle. The person who contracted with you will be working on something else and now you are just an annoyance. There is no downside for them in delay. I have stood at the gate waiting to hear from my administrator that the money hit our bank account before boarding a plane for Colombia. I have never actually missed a flight.

Webinars take much less of your time than a speaking engagement. No travel, no overnight stay in a hotel. There is usually a coordinating call and a few emails to settle on a topic and approve your slides. You may spend some time practicing your 15-30 minute pitch and you have to carve out a two hour slot on your calendar for a one hour webinar and spend additional time promoting the webinar on Twitter and LinkedIn. Charge 1/2 of your daily rate.

If you have never done webinars, I suggest practicing. Walk through your slides while recording yourself. Listen to the recording for signs that you are boring. This is the greatest problem, especially when you have slides in front of you. Your slides should NOT be bullet points. Graphs and images are great. Keep a printout by your side with your key points and ticklers for the great stories you are going to weave into your pitch. Keep the energy level high. Make sure you are using enough inflection in your voice. Listen to radio personalities for examples of what to strive for. Have a glass of water nearby, not coffee or tea, which for some reason are easier to aspirate. One thing that you can bundle with your webinar offer is marketing. Agree to tweet and post to LinkedIn that you are doing the webinar. That may help get attendees. This is when having an extended social network is going to pay off.

Occasionally vendors will want to create a video; usually this is an interview with their CEO, but it could also extend to the equivalent of a video white paper. The final product will be hosted on their web page and YouTube and will include you talking, a client talking about the problem they need solved, and the CTO or CEO talking about the product. Your part of course is to validate the space and the problem. The vendor arranges to have a camera come to you, or, if your house is not a suitable studio, they will have you go to a local studio for your bit. Charge for the full day for this. This used to be a product offering for Gartner, who would also do the production. They charged $70k for each one.

White papers

Writing white papers can be a problem, as you don't want to be branded as another Aberdeen. But white papers often make up a significant amount of your total revenue. Vendors need them to support some claim they are making for their market. They need a powerful third-party voice. But often they won't even approach you unless they know the topic lines up with what you actually believe. One effective technique to avoid directly talking about the vendor's product is to create the white paper with no mention of the vendor at all but include a side bar with the vendor product info. Give them editorial responsibility for that content. Always indicate that "This white paper was sponsored by vendor X" on the bottom. Charge about a half day for each final page. You might spend more than a day with research and the back and forth with the client, but you can also work on the writing while you are traveling.

Market Research Reports

There is a great thirst for market research. Journalists pick up on it and will quote it, hopefully citing their source. Vendors need a third party's estimate of the current market for their Total Addressable Market (TAM) calculations for their business plans. Investors would rather buy a PDF than schedule a call with an industry analyst, although the report often generates such calls for details. You have probably seen market research report teasers if you have Googled "market X size." There is a booming industry in generating slipshod market size reports. I suspect most of them come from the same content factories in India based on their remarkably similar MO. They issue a pseudo press release that somehow gets picked up by Google news so it generates an alert for anyone monitoring a particular industry. When I was at Blancco, one of these issued a "press release" on the global data erasure market. I inquired and received an example PDF with all of the data redacted. But it included a table with the "top players" listed. Blancco, which we believed had 95% of the market for data erasure products, was not even listed. I told the sales contact that I was a little suspicious. Not only did they not list Blancco, but none of the rest of the competitors I tracked were there. Hey presto! They sent me an updated PDF with Blancco listed! I suspect the business model is: identify a market, issue a press release, get a buyer, and churn out a market research report. The asking price is $10,000 for these.

So, create a real market research report. This report should include all the major players and be replete with your take on their offerings, approach to the market, and viability. Include an estimate of total spend on products in the market—the market size. Most importantly, include the projected growth of the market. There are two ways I have identified to do this. First is to look at all the big players in a space, especially the publicly traded ones, and assume that they represent 80% of the market. You just tote up the total reported revenue for the last three years based on annual and quarterly reports of all these vendors and divide by 0.8. You have to do some massaging because not all companies report their results on a calendar year basis.

The second way, and the way I prefer, is to identify all the players in the space and estimate each of their revenue. How do you do that? Private companies will not share that data. But one thing they do not typically control is the LinkedIn profiles of their employees. In most parts of the world, everyone has a LinkedIn profile and they are quick to update it with their current employer. Thus, I have found that when you visit the LinkedIn page for the vendor, the number of employees reported is extremely accurate. All you need to do is estimate the average revenue per employee for the space and multiply that by number of employees and you have a good idea of their revenue.

Note that people are quick to update their profile when they join a company but slow to update when they are laid off. So, for companies that are growing, the number of employees is accurate. For companies that are shrinking, there is a lag.

Produce that market research report. Sell it for something way under $10k. I am targeting $1,500 for the reports I write. Issue a press release. Mention the companies reported on. Then, update the report every quarter with new data and news about changes in the market. Which company was acquired, which had a big funding round, which introduced an innovative product. Then sell annual subscriptions to the research report. Your first recurring revenue stream!

Is that all? Pretty much. But let's look at what a typical year works out to assuming you have settled on a day rate of $5,000.

- 4 retained clients
- 14 speaking engagements
- 6 webinars
- 4 white papers

At $5k a day, you have revenue of $236,800. That is a good start. Just remember that you are paying your salesperson 15% of that! And, really bad news, you have to pay the government a big chunk of that.

To determine your total capacity, assume that you can do two paid engagements a week. At 50 weeks that is 100 days, which at $5k each day is $500k.

What makes it hard to get to that number is the cyclical nature of the business. Most organizations do not do much marketing between May and September. It is summer in the Northern Hemisphere and turnout at speaking events and webinars is low. You would think vendors would think ahead to the next quarter, but the reality is they are so busy with this quarter's activities that they cannot think about the next quarter until the first day of that quarter.

GLG

You may have investment firms and private equity companies reach out directly to engage you. Often a one hour call can turn into an extended engagement. Set your hourly rate high to justify the hassles of writing a proposal or Statement of Work (SOW), invoicing, and collecting.

It is much more convenient to engage the financial community through one of the many services that have arisen in the wake of Enron. Companies like GLG make it possible for an investor to seek out and engage an expert. You, the expert, respond to an inquiry and set your own rate. There is a little friction to get started with these firms. They have to comply with a lot of SEC requirements and will ask you to go through training. They don't want you to share "material non-public" information and they do not want experts who work for the subject companies to violate any employment contracts. Luckily, as an analyst, you rarely are privy to insider information.

GLG filled an important gap for me when I was getting IT-Harvest up and running. It has become much less useful over time. For some reason, the majority of their clients want to speak to people who have bought products from their research subjects. And my chosen rate of $500/hr appears to be on the high end of the range.

Here are the expert network firms I have done work with:
GLG glg.it/council-members/
AlphaSights www.alphasights.com/
Third Bridge www.thirdbridge.com/
Guidepoint www.guidepoint.com/

The best thing about working with these firms is that they are usually fast with payments.

Due diligence for PE and VCs

If your sector experiences a lot of M&A and investment, you should target products for the private equity and venture capital people. Much like stock investors, they tend to follow the crowd and pile into a space when it is hot. Because they are playing with other people's money, they have to justify their investment decisions and they do this through "due diligence," a systematic exercise to demonstrate that they are following a process and not just shooting from the hip. They typically do their own financial due diligence to check that the numbers are correct and they have identified all the risks. This includes reviewing any leases, long term contracts, and liabilities. They may also interview customers to validate the value proposition. But they often need independent validation from industry experts, things like product/market fit, product perception, feature coverage, and a competitive analysis. These are things you can provide.

Your books can generate consulting gigs

Your books can lead to significant opportunities. Ten months after I published *UP and to the RIGHT*, an analyst relations person at McAfee found himself working between Christmas and New Year because Gartner was late in sending out the expected questionnaire for the Magic Quadrant he was responsible for. He told me that he was in the break room at headquarters and found a copy of my book on the shelf. He started reading it and did not go home until he had finished it. He gave that copy to the CMO, who read it on the plane the next day. When she landed, she emailed her entire team and told them to buy the book and expense it. She then reached out to engage me to come in and teach a seminar based on the book to more than 30 people. That one engagement justified all the time I put into the book.

Getting end user clients

The way the influence funnel works requires you to address end users, the consumers of the products sold by the vendors that make up your space. Most of your writing, webinars, and speaking gigs will be addressed to end users. That's how you get the attention of the marketing folks at the vendors.

But what about selling something directly to the end users? Your market research reports may well be the ideal way to offer something to them. It can take over 100 hours to create a market research report. If you calculate that your hourly rate is $500, it means you should generate $50,000 in sales from it to justify the effort. If you priced a report at $1,500, you have to sell 33 copies to justify the work you put into it.

Another product could be a subscription service for end users. That could give them access to your newsletter and a monthly private webinar. Price it low enough so an end user can expense it.

If you have collected a lot of data on the vendors in your space you can create a service that grants access to that data. It could be as simple as a spreadsheet that you send out every quarter or it could be a subscription to an interactive online database.

If you do sell these products, think long and hard about how you are going to prevent the sharing of your data. Make sure the terms of the subscription spell out that the data is for the use of the subscriber only. Watermark PDFs with the recipient's email address. They are not as likely to share it widely knowing that it could end up in public and you will discover they are violating your conditions. Protect an online database with an effective gateway and strong authentication.

The hardest thing for an independent analyst is selling. Since the bulk of your revenue comes from vendors, it feels like a conflict to ask vendors for money when you have to protect your objectivity. You can't turn every vendor briefing into a sales pitch for your services if you want them to perceive you as independent.

These elements of running an independent analyst firm are enough to get you started. As you grow, pay attention to your customers. If one of them asks for something unique, it could give you ideas for repeatable service offerings or new products. After a couple of years of growth, it becomes fun to explore new offerings. Use growth years to prepare for the inevitable hard times on the way to success.

Surviving Hard Times

The greatest risk to any independent analyst is getting wooed by a vendor to join them as a highly-paid executive. The greatest risk to *succeeding* as an independent analyst is an economic downturn. I have worked through four recessions in my career. The first occurred just as I graduated from college in 1982.

The next big downturn occurred in 2000 when the dot-com boom busted. Once again I was lucky to get a job, this time with Gartner. While Gartner was watching expenses closely, it still survived despite the dramatic downturn in the tech space. Gartner signed long-term contracts with its clients, often for three years. To this day they attempt to maintain that practice and they enforce those contracts with vigor. That helps them survive downturns and keep critical staff in the company.

In the fall of 2008 I found myself re-launching IT-Harvest. My friend Leo Cole at Websense asked me to speak at two CISO dinners in New York City. We made reservations at two of the best restaurants in the city and had confirmations from 25 CISOs and Directors from large banks for each dinner. Gene Hodges, the CEO, would preside and I would offer my views on the IT security industry. The dinners were at the Tao Restaurant on Wednesday, September 16, and the next night at the 21 Club. If you have seen *The Big Short*, you may recall the scenes in NYC that week as Lehman Brothers closed its doors on Monday. The Global Financial Crisis had started just as I was getting IT-Harvest off the ground. The dinners were not well attended.

2009 was my most difficult year. Spending by vendors was curtailed immediately as they conserved cash. Marketing dollars are the first to be clawed back during a financial downturn.

As I write this we face a combined crisis of global pandemic and the resultant forecasted economic downturn. Ten million people filed new unemployment claims in two weeks. The government is pumping trillions of dollars into the economy. Surviving the pandemic is the first concern of everyone. Staying in business is the second. Vendors, like all businesses, have closed their offices and required employees to work from home. RSA Conference 2020 was the last major security event to be held before most of the country went on lockdown. IBM, Verizon, and AT&T pulled out in the week before, and the city of San Francisco declared an emergency during the conference. Tens of thousands of attendees went home and into isolation.

VC firm Sequoia issued a warning memo to their portfolio companies on March 5, evoking a feeling of "here we go again," in those who recall Sequoia's famous memo of 2008 titled "R.I.P. Good Times."

I was busy at RSAC launching Security Yearbook 2020 and getting ready for speaking gigs the rest of the "season." By March 4, 2020, every single event for the foreseeable future had been canceled or postponed to the fall.

I could not be happier with the broad acclaim *Security Yearbook 2020* has received. The launch was by far my most successful. But recall that, unless you are Malcolm Gladwell or Michael Lewis, books do not make very much for nonfiction authors. It is speaking engagements and consulting gigs that come from book publishing that can keep you afloat.

Since speaking and consulting gigs are likely to be gone for months, what can I do? Well, one thing I can do is take advantage of the lull to write more. I started posting regularly on Peerlyst, The Analyst Syndicate, LinkedIn, and Forbes.

Being a contributor to Forbes is a great outlet. My columns get tremendous visibility: 90,000 views of *The Demise of Symantec*, so far. I also began exploring my past posts to Forbes. They go all the way back to 2010, when Andy Greenberg (now at *Wired*) invited me to contribute my blog posts.

That gave me the idea to pull together a collection of my writing and turn it into a book. I pulled together *Stiennon On Security: Collected Essays* in record time. At the very least, readers will not have to slog through the clutter of ads and popups that Forbes foists on them.

As I did a first pass edit of 120 columns, I noticed that many of them were inspired by video interviews that I did with founders and executives. With my current interest in the history of our industry (see *Security Yearbook 2020*), I began to think of those 150 interviews as a historical record. I have interviews with Udi Mokady, CEO of CyberArk, Amit Yoran, then CEO of NetWitness, Bill Conner, then CEO of Entrust, and Ruvi Kitov and Reuven Harrison, founders of Tufin. You can still see them all at www.vimeo.com/itharvest.

That led to the idea: why not re-launch the video interviews? The last time I did them was 2016. We reserved a hotel suite in San Francisco and brought in a four-person camera crew to conduct 30 interviews in three days. I have been credited with starting a trend because we were the first at RSAC to do this. Now every security media company offers these. But the actual credit belongs to Phil Alape at Demos-on-Demand. Wouldn't interviews over Zoom serve the same purpose? In addition to executives of established firms, I can interview the founders of a new generation of cybersecurity startups. That will give me plenty of material to write about.

In addition to re-launching the video interview series and publishing volume 1 of my collected essays, I am accelerating the publication of *Curmudgeon*. All these efforts will help IT-Harvest survive the protracted dry spell.

Once again, I have been lucky. I have been successful at establishing IT-Harvest as a trusted source of analytical insights. I finally have no long-term debt. I can get by on savings and the few thousand dollars a month that book sales generate.

Lessons learned

Work to reduce your monthly living expenses while saving enough to get by on for six months. If you have a windfall such as an inheritance or a lucky investment in the stock market, use it to pay down your debt, especially your mortgage. If your children are out of school and it is possible, sell your home and move to a less expensive place. For an analyst, the top requirements for location are proximity to an airline hub and good internet access. Look at income taxes. In the United States, income taxes vary from 10+% in California and Wisconsin down to zero in Florida, Tennessee, Washington, and Alaska. (Income taxes in Alaska can even be negative if you meet residency requirements.) If you net $500k a year you could save as much as $50k by moving from California to Florida.

If you have paid off your mortgage, consider opening a home equity line of credit in case of emergencies like an extended illness or falling off a ladder or a global pandemic.

Have a Plan B. I like to think of scenarios that could impact my business but it never occurred to me that an outbreak of a novel coronavirus could have such an immediate impact.

Thanks to seasonality in the conference and event circuit you will figure out how to survive the dry summer months. Mark Bouchard, who left META Group when Gartner acquired it, figured out that cycle quickly when he set up his own firm. He focused on writing white papers. When he realized the drop in revenue from May to September was just a cycle, he planned extended vacations in the summer.

Focus on selling things that have recurring revenue streams, such as annual retainers, month-to-month consulting gigs, research reports, and subscription services.

Reach out to past clients and ask if you can support them during the financial downturn. Are they looking to generate meaningful content? Can they use a guest blog post? Are they re-thinking their own strategies?

Take advantage of slowdowns to speed up. If everything comes to a complete halt as happened in 2009 and 2020, take the time to increase your output, build your following, and even complete that book project you had to set aside during the busy periods. You could launch your newsletter or start research on a new category in your space. Plan ahead for the inevitable recovery.

The Influence Funnel

Without influence there is no success as an analyst. What is influence and how do you attain it? That is what we will address in this chapter.

Influence is the ability to impact a market. It is when your thoughts, ideas, and vision for the industry push the direction of the vendors and the adaption by end users (companies, universities, government agencies, non-profits, and consumers). At the very least, an influential analyst creates debate from her insights and declarations. That debate is one of the primary indicators of influence. It may appear in the form of bloggers taking you to task, journalists reporting on your contrarian views, even reporting in mainstream media on the consternation that your predications or precautions have engendered.

There are two primary ways to attain the heights of influence, the easy way and the hard way. The easy way is to have a platform from which to speak that, by your very position in the industry, people listen and react to. In politics this is evident when an elected official's opinion on something bears much more weight than all the experts in the world. Celebrities often demonstrate their influence.

Many will recognize my story of how I had some small impact on the IT security space. It is worth retelling because it could only have happened because I was a Gartner analyst. When I joined Gartner in 2000 I was immediately assigned the task of tracking the Intrusion Detection System sector. These IDS systems were generally software running on servers that would tap into the network traffic behind the gateway firewall. Lists of signatures were written that would uniquely identify protocol anomalies, worms, and network-based attacks. When the scanned traffic matched a signature, an alert would be generated and a log entry sent to a repository. After talking to hundreds of companies over three years (see, a day in the life of a Gartner analyst), I realized that every single company I talked to was ignoring those alerts. There were just too many of them. Even Cisco, then the largest vendor of IDS products, had only a small team of five people working regular hours in their IDS group. Obviously there was no great security value in something if you could take off weekends and holidays and be fine with that.

At Gartner's Security and Privacy Summit in June 2003, I made my big pronouncement, which was there was no security value in IDS and Gartner customers should stop spending money on it. I advised that the money would be better spent on technology that actually blocked attacks. It seems obvious now, but back then Intrusion Prevention (IPS) was brand new. Three vendors are credited with inventing the new technology almost simultaneously, which is very common in most technology sectors; when it is time to invent something, the idea occurs to multiple entrepreneurs at once. IPS was the final reinforcement I needed to summon the courage to out an entire segment of my industry.

The Gartner press department took my words, and on the advice of my manager, Vic Wheatman, issued a press release that "IDS is Dead," which put a little sting into it. At the conference I spoke to a standing-room only audience. People were overflowing into the hall and watching me on a monitor. My big pronouncement was accompanied by a slide that said IDS SUCKS, and the audience applauded. You know that you have struck a chord when you get that kind of reaction. Besides, in the ensuing months many people sent me links to articles they had written years before saying the same thing, demonstrating the importance of the platform. This was not some IT security practitioner saying IDS was dead, it was Gartner.

As I walked away from the hall, the CIO of the Pentagon accosted me. He told me that he had heard me say this before and it was high time I came to the Pentagon and addressed his key IT managers. After the physical damage caused by a plane crashing into the Pentagon on 9/11, they were spending huge sums on revamping the networks inside the rebuilt Pentagon, and they had budgeted $160 million for IDS. I told him to name a time and I would be there.

Within a month I was being escorted through the Pentagon to a conference room. On the long walk, the Colonel escorting me said, "Oh, by the way, we invited some other industry experts to the meeting." These other industry experts were the founders and CEOs of all the IDS companies. I had been invited to a debate.

Apparently the only real impact I had on the Pentagon was to change a single letter, D (detection) to P (protection), in the Pentagon's Requests for Proposals. But the lasting impact was that the IDS vendors made great strides in moving from noisy sensing solutions to proactive defensive solutions.

In the meantime, *Network World* magazine issued its list of the 50 Most Powerful People in networking, including my name and crediting the IDS is Dead proclamation. It is always nice to be on a list, especially one that included Bill Gates, John Chambers, and Larry Ellison. That in turn earned me recognition by Gartner at one of their analyst offsite meetings.

Even today people will introduce me as "IDS is Dead" Stiennon. At one of the many social events at the RSA Conference held every year in San Francisco, a sales guy came up to me and said, "Stiennon! I swear when you die they are going to put 'IDS is Dead' on your grave." I replied, "No, they are going to put 'Stiennon is Dead' on my gravestone."

Having a platform is the easy way to have influence. Regardless of where you work, or what your existing platform is, think about the ways you can best leverage it to be influential.

Next, let's talk about the hard way to be influential. It is hard work but keeping at it year after year pays dividends.

How The Influence Funnel Works

There is very little difference between perceived influence and real influence. After all, for the purposes of building your practice, what value is there in being influential and anonymous? So regardless of the impact you have on your industry, followers, and end users, you have to take action to make sure that influence is recognized. You have to practice the methodologies and philosophy expounded in this book. But you also have to do the hard work to ensure that you get credit for your influence.

Perceived influence leads directly to new business. So let's get started.

The influence funnel starts with journalists, which leads to press mentions, which leads to the PR and AR (Analyst Relations) people at vendors, which leads to them engaging you for paying gigs. Along the way you can also be building up your end user client base for your newsletter and advisory service. It all depends on the influence funnel.

One aspect that all influencers share is that they get press coverage. Celebrities, politicians, great thinkers, and academics all benefit from press coverage. If those influencers get quoted and mentioned in the press, and you do, too, then you must be influential.

The top of the influence funnel is represented by journalists. They are your key to influence. An industry analyst must be an expert at press relations. You must get quoted often. Luckily the formula for writing stories about most industries includes a blank for a quote from an objective industry expert. Sadly, most industry reporting of news is generated by press releases. Only a few publications actually dig into stories with the kind of journalism we expect from major publications. The vast majority of the trade press report on news generated by the vendors. Rather than lament this sad state of affairs, look on the bright side. Journalists leave the really insightful writing and reporting to industry analysts! On top of that, the standard formula of news event, quote from news maker, and quote from independent analyst opens the door to press mentions for you, the industry analyst.

How can you get the attention of journalists? That is much easier today than it used to be. Almost all journalists are building their own influence platforms. You can find them on Twitter, LinkedIn, and Facebook. Their email addresses are published next to their stories. We are going to start with those.

First, identify the key journalists in your space. Stack rank them based on the importance (the influence) of their platform. The *Wall Street Journal*, the *New York Times*, *Financial Times*, *Le Monde*, *The Times*, BBC, CNN, and the primary publications in your region all get top ranking, followed by the magazines and websites that are in your specific vertical. Also add bloggers and even other industry analysts to your list. Record their email address, Twitter handle, blog, and other planks in their platforms. Retweet their tweets, comment on their blogs, email them follow up information on the pieces they write. The goal is to be top-of-mind the next time they are writing on your topic area so that they reach out to you.

Eventually, you will recognize when you are on a journalist's short list for commentary. When I first launched IT-Harvest there was one young journalist who had to crank out pieces every day. He would reach out three times a week to get a quote. I always took his call or got back to him via email. If you are unavailable, the journalist will go on to someone else that can help with her deadline. Don't let that happen. Make sure she has your cell phone number.

The ultimate in efficiency is when a quote is lifted from your blog or tweets, so let's address your Twitter presence. Think of any influential person, be it Oprah, Robert Scoble, Guy Kawasaki, or David Sanger at the *New York Times*. They each have a lot of followers, right? (At this writing Oprah Winfrey has 43 million followers; Robert Scoble has 405k; Guy Kawasaki has 1.4 million; and David Sanger has 87.1k.) Regardless of the reality, number of followers is equated with influence. If you reach out to connect with a journalist and she takes the time to look at your Twitter profile what does she see? How many followers do you have? How many tweets?

To succeed as an industry analyst you must use Twitter to your advantage as described earlier. Grow your Twitter following.

From all the care and feeding of your journalist relations, you will get more quotes in the media. If there are articles about your space, the PR people and executives in your space will start to recognize your name. As they build their own influence strategy (probably using the advice I provide in UP *and to the* RIGHT: *Strategy and Tactics of Analyst Influence*) they will be reminded to include you in their press release distribution and they will reach out to you when they are looking for someone to write a white paper or participate in a speaking gig or webinar.

Vendors will also reach out to ask for quotes they can use in their press releases. PR people know the formula too and strive to make it easy for journalists to write a complete story just from the press release, so an analyst quote is important. If they support your position on their space they will even ask if you will be willing to speak to journalists who may be writing about their news. Always say yes. You may end up being quoted in several news sources on the same story. When the producers of NPR or the BBC are looking for someone to interview, your name will be the obvious choice.

The Vendor Briefing

Once you are perceived as influential, you will find your inbox flooded with briefing requests. Accept them all. This is the next step in the funnel. For the executives and marketing team to schedule an hour of their time to brief you is a big time commitment. (For them, you have all the time in the world. Basically you have to get busy before you get productive in terms of money coming in the door.)

During the briefing is where many analysts fall down on the job. They learned the wrong lesson in Curmudgeon 101. Somewhere they picked up the idea that trashing vendors is a good way to succeed. They never took a moment to realize that the industry can get along very well without analysts, but that there would be no industry without vendors. Analysts provide clarity, direction, insight, and help to educate end users about the drivers and disrupters in the industry. My approach is that every vendor with customers has something. And if those customers come back every year and buy more, there is no better validation that the vendor is on to something.

Do your homework. Check the website of the vendor. Look at their recent news announcements. Study the bios of the executives. Check them out on LinkedIn (they may even notice because often you can see who has looked at your LinkedIn profile).

During the briefing there are two rules: listen and ask questions. They have been raked over the coals by the Gartner analyst who wants to pigeonhole them, and thus put them in the Niche Quadrant of the Magic Quadrant. If your reaction to their baby is that they are wrong and have to change everything to conform to your picture, they will dismiss you. If you don't get it, why should they waste any more effort on you?

Next up, give them ideas. Invariably you will see a connection between what they do and what another vendor does. Offer to make introductions. Or you may have an end user client whose needs fit what the vendor is offering. Make that introduction, too. One of the primary values of industry analysts is their role as a connector. They have a near-complete picture of all the players in the industry, and they are great resources for headhunters. I had one vendor client that was looking for a new CTO. They had received 200 resumes from a retained headhunter and interviewed 40. I introduced the CEO to two good friends that were a fit. They hired the first one they interviewed and sent me three bottles of fine wine. You may ask, "Wait, a headhunter's fee is at least 20% of the first year's salary, shouldn't you have charged for that service?" But think about it. If I charged to find candidates for a position, I would do what any headhunter does: send over hundreds of resumes, hoping that one of them sticks. As an industry analyst, my recommendations carry a lot of weight *because* I am not getting compensated.

You can offer suggestions on how to improve the messaging in the briefing deck or other material. You don't have to show false enthusiasm, but if their solution gets you excited, convey that.

Avoid a sales pitch during the briefing. Let your salesperson do a follow up call. If they do ask about what services you offer go ahead and tell them, but leave pricing to sales.

Try to schedule breaks between briefings so that you can jot down notes while they are fresh. Write down your initial thoughts on the product and the people. File those away so they are easy to find in the future. You could put them in your CRM system too so the salesperson (team?) can see them. Write a short paragraph you may use later when you are called on to write about their sector.

Speaking

If I had to rank the value of the many activities an analyst engages in, I would put writing first and public speaking second. In this chapter we will review how to speak in public as well as how to build your speaking business.

Like writing, good public speaking can be learned. All it takes is practice. You will find as your influence grows, so will opportunities to speak at conferences, vendor seminars, road shows, and customer events.

At first, unpaid speaking gigs at conferences are a great way to increase your influence and exposure. Eventually you will be asked to keynote conferences for a fee, plus travel expenses. But in the beginning, you will be responding to requests for speakers issued by conferences. Identify all the conferences in your industry. Include even the ones overseas. Those can be the most valuable to attend and spread your network beyond your place of origin. Get on the conference mailing lists so you see the announcements. Keep an eye open for new conferences. Often you can find conferences by examining the web pages of the vendors you follow. They will post the conferences at which they are exhibiting. Get your salesperson to reach out to see if the vendor wants to brief you face-to-face at the conference. If you are speaking, they will definitely want to meet with you. You want to be seen everywhere.

Develop several slide decks that you think are of value. Your pitches can be of the industry overview type, or they can be on changes to the industry including drivers, disrupters, inhibitors, and recent M&A activity. Before submitting to any conferences, write down a synopsis of your pitch, key takeaways, and five questions that will be answered for attendees. Eventually your speaking agent will need these to sell you as a paid speaker. Develop a speaker's bio, a short one of 150 words, and a longer one of 500 words. List the events you have presented at in the past, and the publications you have been quoted in, and your book, of course. Also compile the links to any speaking gigs that have recorded videos of you presenting.

A good presentation

There are dozens of books written on professional speaking. I can distill them all to "tell a good story." Storytelling is the first formalized method of human communication. We are hardwired to listen to stories. Most analysts I have met are either natural storytellers or they have acquired the skill from being an analyst for so long.

Your presentation can either be a single story interlaced with your subject matter or a series of stories. If a presentation is just a recital of facts, observations, and insights, an attendee will walk out unable to even recall what it was about. The parts they do remember will be the stories they heard, even if they were an aside to the main point.

A great way to start a pitch is with the phrase "Let me tell you a story." You will have the audience's immediate attention. Their minds go into story reception mode. They are looking for characters, plot, and a good ending. That is just where a presenter wants her audience. All you have to do is deliver.

You can tell a personal story: how you became aware of a problem, how you confronted it, how you solved it, and lessons you learned.

Or you can tell someone else's story. The story of the founder of your industry (Billy Durant in automotive, for instance) tied to your topic/message would be well received. Can you tie your pitch to the history of your industry? If so, mention names and personalities.

A good speaker can deliver an enthralling 45-minute presentation with no slides. But slides are usually expected and they are a great takeaway. The conference organizers often make them available and they have your contact information in them, so it is very important to take advantage of that. Post your slides to SlideShare, too, in order to extract the benefit of extended exposure to your topic. Remember that SlideShare is owned by LinkedIn, so prospects for future speaking gigs will see your presentations. Thus, you need to build slide decks.

Enough has been written about Death by PowerPoint for the message to have sunk in by now. Think of your slide deck as illustrating your story or stories and avoid bullet points. Collect images of the people, events, and things that make up your story. Of course, graphs are great; most audiences expect graphs of some sort from industry analysts. Don't disappoint them. If you are delivering a pitch about your industry, you could probably dwell for 90% of the time on one graph, though expanding the graph into detailed sections as you talk about them would serve to alleviate the visual boredom. At Gartner, the Magic Quadrant for a sector often serves this purpose.

Developing your own style of delivery comes with time and practice. Practice your pitch alone several times, always focusing on the transitions you will use from slide to slide. You don't want to have a pattern of: view slide, talk about slide, advance the slide, look at the slide, etc. You want the slides to be illustrating your story so the transitions should be smooth.

When you first start your public speaking career, look for opportunities to present the same topic many times. After a dozen times presenting the same pitch in front of an audience you will start to feel the fluidity that comes with repetition. Being in front of an audience gives you a chance to pick up on subtle cues that let you know what works and what doesn't. The pacing before a quip, or punchline, can make all the difference in audience reaction. The easy flow to the big finish can only be evolved through this repetition.

Find a local meeting that is looking for a luncheon speaker. Create a video of yourself presenting. Take time to write your speech down. Other than very formal situations you will rarely read a speech, but it is valuable to have a written document. It helps you identify the awkward or cumbersome lines, or the ones you stumble over. You can practice those lines over and over to get them to flow smoothly, or you can rewrite them to be less problematic. Many times the process of writing generates new thoughts and insights, too.

You can post the written speech to your blog and embed your SlideShare deck. That way the search engines will find your topic and help your SEO. Record yourself reading the speech, even publish it as a podcast, or create a recorded webinar along with your slides.

Post Performance Crash

Over time you will learn to relish the speaking experience. There is a performance rush of endorphins from being on stage, from getting a reaction out of the crowd, of stepping down into a small crowd of people anxious to meet you and exchange business cards. But beware the post-speech let down that many public speakers (and performers) experience. It can take two forms: just the letdown from the endorphin rush when the pitch went well, or the depression that hits you if you feel it did not go well. Have a plan for activities the rest of the day that will give you something to think about right away. It could be a scheduled call with a journalist, or a briefing with a vendor. If you know someone in town, have a meeting scheduled to catch up. Collapsing in your hotel room with room service and Netflix may be a a justifiable reward for a job well done, but I have found that it does little to eliminate the letdown. Doing something productive does.

Getting Beyond Failure

There will be failures. Every public speaker has them. I once put together a pitch that went counter to all of the accepted wisdom of the IT security industry. I made the argument that risk management is worthless for IT security. The first time I presented it, the conference organizers had specifically asked me to deliver an opening keynote that would get people talking the rest of the three day gathering. It worked and I received a lot of positive feedback. The next time I presented it though, things did not go well. It was a keynote for a risk management conference and the person who introduced me even had the title VP Risk Management. The most she could say about my presentation was that it was "interesting," and not a single person accosted me in the hallway to either refute my thesis or offer their support. Learn from these failures. Matching the pitch to the audience is one thing I have learned.

A disaster that I still cringe over came when I was still learning the speaking business. I was a Gartner analyst and a big vendor client had contracted with Gartner for me to keynote their annual sales kick-off meeting. I had a new slide deck which I had never practiced. I was supposed to speak for 45 minutes and take questions for another 15. I flew through the entire deck in ten minutes and the organizers were thrown into disarray. The host had to tell everyone to take the mid-morning break for coffee while they hunted down the next presenter. Since then I am glad to report that I have developed an uncanny sense of timing. I often hit the allotted time within a minute.

   Like many speakers, I cannot watch a clock or timer when I speak. I do not recommend it because a look at a clock can derail you when you are on a roll. You may stutter or lose momentum. What I do is have a particular slide in every deck that I can speak to for an hour if pressed. When I get to that slide, I can give the short version or the extended version with asides and multiple stories attached.

   Every speaker has encountered technical problems with microphones, projectors, or issues with the slide decks loading. Take these in stride. Be professional. Don't fiddle around with stuff. You want to avoid sucking the audience into your frustration with technology. If a technical crew is present, request that they come up on stage while you start. Step away from the podium. Maybe step down into the audience. Start your introduction if the problems look like they are going to be extended. Deliver it without slides. If you can speak loud enough, you can even do without a microphone in many instances.

   I was once on the road for an extended time and had to get to San Jose for a presentation. On the way my laptop died. I dropped by the local Gartner office and picked up a replacement and loaded my presentation on it before heading to the venue downtown. When I got there I jumped on stage to plug in the replacement laptop only to discover it had no VGA port for connecting to the projector. No worries. I had given this particular presentation many times and could practically see the slides in my head. The presentation got a warmer welcome in that situation than it ever had.

Impromptu Speaking

Sometimes you will be asked to speak at the last minute. You may have been invited to sit on a panel at a conference and a keynote speaker failed to show up. Or the audience reaction was so positive at your morning keynote that you are asked to do the wrap up keynote, too. If you have a few minutes before jumping on stage, quickly write down the topic, hopefully one you have spoken about before, and then write down cues for a series of stories you can tell. Then write down the key takeaways. Working off of a list is always a great way to organize a pitch. Begin by saying, "I have only four points I want to make today." Then proceed to make the points and tell your stories.

In a similar vein, sometimes you will be asked to present someone else's topic, maybe even using their slides. Do not do it. Instead, stand up and deliver your own pitch. Perhaps provide some transition to warn the audience. "Good morning! Instead of addressing the problems with our industry, I am going to talk about the opportunities and the future that faces us." I learned this lesson when I once filled in for another Gartner analyst who was scheduled to present on Risk Management at a conference in Cleveland. She could not make it and Cleveland was an easy stop on the way back to my home airport of Detroit Metro. I reviewed her slides on the plane, landed in Cleveland, grabbed a taxi, and made it to the conference at 9:10 a.m., only ten minutes late. Talk about being rushed. It was probably the most boring pitch I have ever given. I tried to find interesting things to say about each bullet point on each slide. I felt sorry for the audience. Maybe this is why I don't like Risk Management.

Other Dos and Don'ts

- Do speak with authority. You are the industry analyst. You know your topic. You know your industry. You are the authority.
- Do speak with energy. This is the one piece of constructive feedback that I have received that I think of every time I get on stage. My manager at Gartner offered it after my first time at the Big Show, Gartner's annual IT Symposium and Expo at Disney World in Florida. The smallest audience is 500 people. (I never got to address the full audience of 8,000.) It was my first time and I presented a dry summary of the IT security space. Since then, I fight to keep the energy level high. You have probably heard of the advice to get over stage fright: pretend your audience is sitting in their underwear. I do the opposite, I imagine everyone's nightmare: getting on stage underdressed. A little nervousness adds to the energy level. Use inflection in your voice.
- Do speak directly to audience members. In the first few minutes of any presentation, scan the audience and pick out the faces that are alive and engaged. (Try not to think about the few faces that have that stunned, post-prandial stupor showing.) Find one on each side of the stage and make eye contact. Your energy levels will feed off of each other.
- Do try to meet the audience beforehand. I try to talk to a few during the breaks, or as they are gathering in the hall. It helps set you at ease and you may get more insight into why they have come to the event.

- Do be aware of local mores and culture. The most disastrous pitch I ever witnessed was given in Orlando. The famous internet security pioneer who presented felt it necessary to begin by explaining his atheism and anti-state stance. I counted 33 people that were so offended that they walked out on his presentation.
- Don't drink coffee starting an hour before your pitch. Coffee is great for increasing your energy levels, but for many people it can have harmful effects on their voice. I switch to tea beforehand.
- Don't visit the restroom just before getting on stage. It is natural to feel the call when you are nervous. Especially if you have been drinking tea. But accidents happen, and they happen at the most inopportune moments; like right before you get on stage.
- Don't hang out in front of the room prior to your pitch. After your sound check and review of your slides to make sure they are the right ones, step to the back of the room or sit in the front row. Don't come forward until you are introduced, or the doors have closed and your time has arrived.
- Don't ever refer to your audience as "you people." I was once at an event in Mexico City and watched aghast as a fellow analyst repeatedly referred to the audience as "you people down here." Be inclusive.
- Don't try to be a member of the tribe you are speaking to. Many speakers try to establish that they know their audience with a preamble about the first time they were in that particular region or city. This always comes off as superficial and condescending. Being there is a strange experience for the presenter perhaps, but the audience lives there.
- Don't lecture. Yes, you have to speak with authority. But pull the audience in with inclusive language. "We" instead of "you."

It's Up to You

There are some things that may depend on the situation or your personal preference.

To stand behind the podium or wander around? If you read a lot of the books on public speaking, you are often encouraged to wear a lavaliere and walk out into the audience. I have seen this done by John Chambers, then CEO of Cisco, to great effect. Of course, he had a very carefully choreographed presentation with eight "confidence monitors" set up throughout the room, so he could always see his slides. I have seen other great presenters walk around with a hand mic and ask the audience questions. Those techniques are beyond me, but they may fit your style or the situation may demand it. I prefer to stay on stage and not move around very much. I even like standing behind a podium when I want to use my stentorian voice, as opposed to my usual conversational voice.

Jokes. After several attempts at telling jokes, I have decided they are not for me. Sure a quip here and there or a sarcastic jibe may be called for, but I am terrible at delivering jokes. If you are comfortable telling jokes or have had training at Second City or Comedy Castle, go for it. Otherwise ignore the advice that many old guides to public speaking give. Leave jokes to comedians.

Another language. I have been at many conferences where I am the only presenter in English. I think the audience appreciates it if you are familiar with their language and you greet them in it. But unless you are as fluent in a second language as your primary one, I would avoid trying to deliver the whole presentation in another language. Sitting through any presentation can be a painful experience, but one spoken in a language not native to the presenter can be excruciating.

Speaking with a translator. Many conferences will provide simultaneous translation. My experience has always been positive, but keep in mind a few things:

- Go over your slides with the translator beforehand to clarify any questions about the industry-specific terms you will be using.
- Avoid idioms. They will not translate well.
- Humor definitely will not come across.
- Be aware of the lag in translation. Give the translator time to complete the last thing you said before advancing your slides.
- The Q&A session usually works. You don your headset and wait for the translator to provide the question. Then you answer and wait for the translator to finish. Remember that many in the audience understand you at least as well as the translator.
- Audiences in Japan can be the hardest to address. They are famous for not having any questions during the Q&A session. Come prepared with some questions that the moderator can ask you.

Building a Speaking Practice

Paid speaking is one of the primary income streams of a successful industry analyst. At my busiest I did 50 paid speaking engagements a year. There may be independent analysts who do that much speaking, but you can imagine that would be a full-time job unless you had a lot of support. Mind you, the fees for speaking do not flow back to the analysts at the big firms. It is just part of the job.

There are several opportunities for paid speaking gigs as an industry analyst:

Internal meetings. Most large vendors ($40 million in revenue and up) have an annual sales kick off meeting. They might even have several, one in each major region: Americas, EMEA, AsiaPac. They often hire an outside speaker to address the sales teams. The desired topic is usually an overview of the industry and its prospects. A prominent industry analyst is perfect for these events. Aside from the fee you collect, it is also a great opportunity to get an inside peek at their sales operations. You also have a chance to interact with key executives which serves to solidify your relationship with the vendor. Make sure, when you put your presentation together, to think of impressing the field sales team. It may occur to them to bring you in to address prospects at their local events. Another opportunity is to speak at vendors' Customer Advisory Board (CAB) meetings. These are even more informative than sales kickoffs. You get to meet the buyers and advocates of the vendor's products. It is a great time to dig into their likes, concerns, and hopes for the product roadmap.

Sales events. Most vendors have set aside market development funds (MDF), usually 2-3% of sales, which are reinvested with the distributors and resellers on various marketing programs. This could include local advertising and sponsorship of events, often a booth at a local trade show. One way those funds can be spent is on bringing in paid speakers (you) to address a breakfast, lunch, or dinner seminar. The usual formula is to use your name and topic to draw the audience. You can help drive additional attendees by broadcasting the upcoming event to your vast social media following that you have been working so hard to build. You speak for 30 minutes, and the local sales rep speaks the rest of the time. The best salespeople plan these events a quarter in advance and follow up on leads they generate throughout the following months.

It can be complicated to land this type of speaking gig. Often corporate marketing, channel marketing, and the event team from the distributor need to get involved. And sadly, they are often flops due to lack of support from the field. I have gained lots of experience talking to empty rooms. One road show, hosted by a major vendor in the digital certificate space, was scheduled for six cities. In most of the cities, the audience consisted of a few employees of the vendor and one or two non-decision makers at potential prospects. Treat every speaking opportunity the same though, regardless of how well it is attended. When I joined Webroot Software in 2004, they made big plans for my first appearance at a Gartner event. They paid the large fee to reserve a vendor speaking slot and handed out fliers to "come hear the former VP Research speak." My pitch was late in the afternoon in a meeting room with chairs set for 500 people. There was one attendee, a friend. I delivered my pitch as if the room was full. There weren't many questions at the end.

Sponsored conference slots. Many conferences, especially regional ones, sell sponsorship packages to vendors that include a speaking slot. The vendor may realize that the audience may not want to hear another product pitch during a luncheon keynote and their own executives may not be available, so they will pay to have an analyst present on their behalf. They get the benefit of the "Lunch Keynote Sponsored By..." signage and any good reaction engendered by your speech may accrue to the vendor.

Road shows are the best. A vendor schedules a series of events across the world for a new initiative or product launch. They leverage the same material to promote each event. They support the local field with email blasts and a registration page. Roadshows are great for you because you get to deliver the exact same pitch over and over. By the third or fourth time, you have honed your delivery. Your timing is spot on. Your energy and fluidity is compelling. And you get paid for each one. I seek out road shows and will discount my fees by 50% for four or more appearances.

After your book is published, another world of speaking opportunities opens up. Authors are popular subject matter experts that often speak to audiences outside their industry-specific events. You may be an industry analyst that covers the emerging drone industry, or 3D printing, or telematics and self-driving cars. New technology areas can be of interest to a much wider audience and you will find that you are in demand at conferences and business meetings you never knew existed. It is at this point that finding a speaking agent, in addition to your salesperson, will be valuable.

Most highly paid speakers have whole teams of people to manage their speaking engagements. Your agent will negotiate the fee and travel arrangements, including the requirement to pay a portion of the fee up front. Remember the importance of cash flow; you do not want to be traveling all over the world accumulating a hefty accounts receivable balance.

In addition to negotiating your fee, a speaking agent can help to make sure the whole process goes smoothly for you. She gets a signed contract, ensures that you have directions to the hotel the night before, even arranges with the client to have a car and driver pick you up.

You may have seen speakers bureaus websites. Speakers bureaus are not worth talking to until after you are a sought-after speaker. They will do nothing to promote you and get you new business. They typically host a catalog of speakers and act as an agent only for incoming requests, usually generated by you, the speaker. Your agent can maintain a relationship with multiple speakers bureaus just to make them aware that you are there in case they ever get a request for an expert in your space.

The National Speakers Association can be of immense value to someone starting out in the business. They maintain a great Facebook page which is open to non-members that I highly recommend. Most of the NSA members are in the category of motivational speaker; they speak on some personal tragedy and their battle to overcome it, or they coach people in how to build a business using their methods. As such, they typically demand much lower fees than an industry analyst, rarely over $10k and usually closer to $2k. But these speakers make up for the low fees in the number of engagements they get, often speaking to schools, professional societies, and smaller meetings. They tend to be very good speakers with vast experience, so you can learn a lot from them. In addition to the NSA, Toastmasters and Dale Carnegie courses can help a speaker get comfortable with addressing crowds.

The Analyst's Life

What is a day in the life of an industry analyst like? They are all different. There are days devoted to researching and writing. Days with multiple vendor briefings. Unscheduled calls from retained clients with strategy questions sparked by a major acquisition in their space. And constant work building your social media presence. Or you may be on the road to participate in a speaking or strategy session. These are just a few of the daily activities.

Research. In order to form the foundation of your research, you need to discover all of the vendors of products in your field. Along the way you will find the consultants, resellers, distributors, and publications in your space, too. But the vendors are paramount. Say you are starting from ground zero, perhaps with a new category of vendors you have not covered before. Create a spreadsheet with columns for company name, website, LinkedIn URL, number of employees according to LinkedIn, street address, city, state, and country of the headquarters.

Find vendors by starting with all of the conferences about your space. The sponsors and exhibitors will likely be vendors you should track. Add them to your spreadsheet. Go to CrunchBase and search on your segment to discover vendors that have received funding but are not yet exhibiting at conferences. While you are there, record how much total funding they have received. You can search the internet, too. Perhaps someone has already published a list. These are however often woefully out of date, or the person who created them did not have the same requirements for inclusion that you do.

When you are confident you have most of the vendors, reach out on LinkedIn and try to connect to key people: the CEO, CMO, and Analyst Relations person. Request a briefing from the AR person.

Search Google News about each of the vendors to see they last time they appeared in the press. You may only find press releases, but look at those to get a feel for the vendor's momentum. There will be announcements of new funding, new products, key hires, events they are sponsoring, and acquisitions they are making. Record the name of the press contact at the bottom of the press release. These are key people for you.

Writing. You will probably be writing every day. During the week, even when you are on an airplane, you should be writing your next column or blog post. I keep a Scrivener project open for my blog posts. I create a new folder for every topic I want to write on and create a stub of 150 words just to remind me of the topic and the point I am trying to make. Throughout the week I drop in links to articles and quotes. Then when I am ready to crank out a column, I can just write it without having to do as much research. Carve out big chunks of time, probably on Saturday and Sunday, for your big projects: a white paper, your next research report, or your next book.

Briefings. You could have as many as five briefings a day scheduled. Here is what I wrote about briefings in *UP and to the RIGHT*. Keep in mind this is the advice for the vendor to follow and deals mostly with influencing a Gartner analyst.

> It does not cost anything to brief an analyst. A lot of vendors don't realize this, but the savvy ones do. The vetting process is more stringent than for an inquiry. You have to fill out a briefing request and send it in. You should know beforehand which analysts you want on the call; if you appeal to more than one, you may get several on the call. A briefing is a rare opportunity to get a full hour of an analyst's time, but do not read a bunch of bullet points to an analyst. Don't forget she has a full work load. If you don't keep her engaged, she will be doing email and filling in her report from the previous call.
>
> Typically you will have the AR person and a product person on the phone. The more senior the product person, the better. The CEO is even better if you are still a single product vendor. No matter who it is, they should be good at briefings. That means conversant with the product and used to handling questions and objections ("That's a great question, we have thought long and hard about that and here is what we came up with...").
>
> Just as I described in the section on SAS days, the presentations should be professional. Not a lot of bullet points but lots of data. And keep the number of slides down. You try sitting through four to six briefings a day and see how you feel at the end of a day of slide presentations.

Now, some pointed advice on those slide presentations. Send your slides to the analyst beforehand. Do not even bother scheduling a Webex or other online presentation. The analyst is not necessarily sitting at her desk. She may be at the gate waiting for a flight or in a hotel room with no Internet access. You will see why the analyst likes to have the slides as soon as you start the presentation. She will interrupt to ask you to skip ahead to what you do. She will stipulate the existence of the problem. No need to go through the slide with the graph that goes up exponentially to the right, or the slide with the headlines from the papers, or the survey results that demonstrate nine out of ten CIOs agree. If you do include those slides, be prepared for that interruption. It is the analyst's favorite trick. But it is not spiteful; she has seen all those slides a hundred times. She has created slides like that and even includes them in her own presentations. You are talking to the expert on the problem and the solution. Get to your solution. I recommend starting out with the 'who we are' slide that lists the top salient points. Who are your founders/key people? Where are you located? What do you do? How big are you (sales, revenue, etc.)? Let her pigeonhole you. It's the way an analyst's brain works. It has to be that way considering the amount of data and the number of vendors she talks to. The very next slide should be a big, beautiful picture of your product. If it is a hardware product, this is great. If it is software or a service, it is harder. Figure that out. You will need that picture for lots of other reasons anyway.

Now dive into how your product works: what components, what features, speeds, and feeds. Analysts love data. Have I said that before?

Pay attention to the questions the analyst poses. Answer honestly and professionally.

By way of example, let me tell you about the briefing from hell. A very big technology company (and a very big Gartner client) scheduled a briefing with four analysts in the security group to introduce them to the huge effort they were launching in the security space: security professional services. We got on the call and were exposed to a seventy-page PowerPoint. It went on, and on, and on. There was no data, only bullet points about how well positioned the company was to offer consulting services. The four analysts were all on AOL Instant Messenger during the briefing and our chat messages were less than complimentary. We colluded on who would ask what question to trip them up. We took turns putting ourselves on mute and getting up to go to the bathroom. It was a miserable and memorable moment. From that time on I refused to have anything to do with that vendor. I would not take calls from them and I made sure I was not available

for their big analyst day or SAS engagements. Don't be that vendor. I never heard anything more of their professional services effort. It probably never got off the ground—they killed it with a PowerPoint presentation.
Every briefing should accomplish four goals:
1. Build a relationship
2. Form the overall opinion of your company
3. Gather intelligence on what the analyst is looking for
4. Plant a tagline in the analyst's brain

Build a relationship

Every interaction with the analyst builds on your relationship, but the briefing is a structured opportunity to establish a communication bond. It is important to identify who is going to represent the company to the analyst. Contact consistency is key. If a different person briefs the analyst each time, they are not going to know anyone at your company at all. There are two separate bonds to create, the bond with the AR person and the bond with the product person.

The AR person is going to quickly get on a first name basis with the analyst. She/he is the communicator, one who knows the company's message, people, and business, but not necessarily the ins and outs of the product. Not being technical is fine. The analyst does not expect the AR person to answer questions on product details, but the AR person is an excellent facilitator. This is the person who arranges all the briefings and inquiries and is on all the calls. If the analyst ever has a question, you want him to feel he can reach out directly by email, and eventually, by phone to the AR person. The AR person must get back to him as quickly as possible with the answer. Always cite the source when doing so. Mention by name the CEO, CTO, or product specialist that provides the answer. Always build on the analyst's understanding of who your company is.

The AR person must attend events at which the key analysts are present. Build on the relationship by associating a face/personality with the name and voice on the phone. Schedule a breakfast meeting to include the AR person, the analyst, and the CEO or product specialist.

Get to know the analyst. What are his interests? He will have a lot. I have found that analysts may not be the warmest creatures but they have varied interests and usually more than one area of expertise. He may be a marathon runner, or skier, or engage in adventure travel. He may be a ham radio enthusiast, or collector of some arcane art objects. He may dream of being a cooper. (I am thinking of an analyst friend whose dream of making barrels coincides with my interest in distilling whisky.)

Analyst personalities come in all types. Some are aloof, some are full of themselves, some are meek and nerdy. For the most part they do not excel at people skills. If they did, they probably would have become managers or executives. When getting to know an analyst, keep in mind that all analysts are experts, and they know it. They are extremely confident on their home turf—their area of expertise. That is why they respond so well to questions. They know the answers and they revel in providing them. Often that confidence leaks over into other fields that they are not experts in: politics, health, the economy. Continue to feed their need and ask questions about those topics as well.

There is a certain class of analysts who treats vendors with scorn. I think it is because they became analysts before they were experts in a field. For a period in the late '90s Gartner experimented with hiring writers and journalists, sometimes right out of school. The idea was that as the company grew, they would not be able to afford to hire the experts in every field. They wanted to create a business model that did not rely on finding and retaining rock stars. After all, having the Gartner Analyst title should be enough to establish the credentials of an analyst. Of course, since writing and communicating are such important qualities for an analyst, many of these writer and journalist recruits turned into superb analysts. But along the way, many of them picked up on the wrong attitudes. Analysts are selected for stubbornness as I pointed out, and they are trained to be contrarians—curmudgeons. When they are new to Gartner, they sit in on a lot of analyst calls and briefings to learn the ropes. When they see the senior analyst being harsh to a vendor they begin to assume that is what makes a good analyst. And, let's face it, the most controversial and reputation-building successes an analyst may be known for is his or her criticism of a market-leading vendor. The novice picks up on this and thinks that vendor-bashing is the essence of being an analyst. In truth, this is very wrong. A senior analyst who came from industry realizes that the space they cover was created by vendors. All of the innovation and forward movement comes from vendors. Because, after all, the vendors are the only ones that have more contact with end users than the analysts do. Their products are the result of many iterations of responding to customer requests for modifications or feature enhancement. Savvy analysts will still beat up the vendors, but will exhibit much more respect than the younger breed of analyst.

If your analyst is one of these vendor-bashers, be comforted that the rest of the vendors in your space get the same harsh treatment. You just have to do a better job of managing your analyst than your competitors.

During briefings is when you also build the connection between the analyst and your product expert. Your expert may be the technical founder of your company if you are still small and growing, or it may be the product engineer or manager if you are a large, established firm. It should not be the product marketing person. It has to be someone who works on developing the product, who knows the code it is written in and who works with customers on product issues; in short, the technical owner of the product. This person will probably be more technical than the analyst and thus command respect. If he or she is also a well-known name in the industry from previous successes or work in the open source community, all the better.

Make sure the product expert understands the complete strategy for analyst influence. Share the goal and the plan. Get him or her to understand the importance of analyst influence. Give him a copy of this book. Stress that there are things that can be learned from the analyst.

The product expert should be shepherded by the AR contact who will work to create opportunities to strengthen the bond with the analyst. Any white papers the product expert has written, or videos he or she has produced, should be shared with the analyst. The more the expert can teach the analyst the better. The AR person will arrange the breakfast or dinner with the analyst at conferences. The product expert will convey the excitement of what he/she is working on.

If the product expert is not a fluid communicator, that is okay. Certainly fluidity and comfort comes with practice, maybe a little training, but the analyst will cut him some slack. They deal with geeks within their client base all the time.

Form the overall opinion of your company

The second purpose of the briefing is to convey a solid understanding of what your company is (ability to execute) and what your company does (completeness of vision). This might be hard if you are HP or Yahoo! right now. If the company is not even sure of where they are heading and what business they are in, the analyst will pick up on that. If you have a complicated message and a complicated go-to-market strategy, simplify. Make the image of your company easy to fit into the Magic Quadrant you are targeting.

By way of illustration: your company has a complete suite of office productivity tools, from word processing to financial planning to integrated voice-text-video. The analyst, however, only covers word processors and is gathering data for the next MQ on word processors. Don't depict your company as one that has dozens of perfectly integrated tools of which word processing is a small part. Paint your company as a word processing company that has built dozens of ancillary products that feed into the word processor. See what that does? Your disjointed scope is transformed into demonstrable completeness of vision!

This example may seem like a stretch on my part to make a point. But talk to Fortinet if you want a real world example. They built a new security platform that is not only a firewall, but incorporates the features of products that reside in as many as eight different Magic Quadrants. When they make a pitch to get included in the MQ on Secure Web Gateways (the devices that prevent you from going to malicious or inappropriate web sites from work), they are told "only purpose-built Secure Web Gateways are allowed in the MQ. You have a multi-purpose device so it can't be included." Imagine the frustration. Fortinet has more Secure Web Gateways deployed than any of the vendors in the MQ, but is not included!

Gather intelligence on what the analyst is looking for. It is during the briefing that you are going to be exposed to how the analyst thinks about the space. Try to understand that as clearly as you can. Ask questions for clarity. This intelligence is going to inform all of your future communication with the analyst. She thinks that growth in number of resellers is a key indicator of ability to execute? Make sure she knows about every major reseller you sign up and the upward trend in numbers of resellers. Ask her to define completeness of vision. Is it a spread of products across consumer-SMB-Enterprise? Is it a particular feature? A cloud strategy? Scalability? Your competitors who are already in the Leaders Quadrant should have all the qualities she mentions. If they don't, ask how they became Leaders. Take what you learn and stress these areas of development in future briefings. If you are missing one of the requirements that demonstrate completeness of vision, come up with a strategy to get there. This is vision after all, you don't necessarily have to have the feature—just the plan to get there.

Plant a tagline in the analyst's brain

Have you seen the movie Inception? Leonardo DiCaprio is challenged to take on the hardest task of all: plant an idea in someone's head that he thinks is his own. That is what you have to do in the briefing, without the benefit of a dream-making machine. Start small with implanting a tagline. I can tell you that by the end of a busy week of briefings, I cannot remember what the vendor I talked to on Monday even does without referring to my notes. At the minimum you want to implant a memory in the analyst's brain of who you are (your company name) and what you do.

"We are iKangaru, the marsupial tracking software company." In the strange way the world works, the very next week a Gartner client will call to inquire about marsupial tracking software. If you have done your job, the analyst will spend half an hour talking about your products.

That's the easy part; the next task is much more difficult. You want to plant the seed of what makes you different. What about your company might force the analyst to re-think his own assumptions about completeness of vision in his MQ? "We are the only marsupial tracking company to realize that all marsupials have pouches." If you accomplish this you are the de-facto visionary. Now all you have to work on is ability to execute.

Think long and hard about what you want to surgically implant in the analyst's brain. Going back in and removing it or replacing it may be impossible. Ideas are like cancer; they grow.

The best possible way to implant an idea is to create that "inception" moment. Give the analyst all the information she needs to come up with the idea on her own. Often you will be able to tell. The tone of the briefing changes. The analyst "gets it." She starts asking clarifying questions. If you are a client, she may even state it for you: "Hey, you are the only vendor in the space that actually uses pouches for marsupial tracking!" Your job is done.

That excerpt was written for the AR team. Now here is what you need to know about being on the receiving end of a briefing.

In preparation for the briefing, the analyst relations or PR person will ask what specific questions you may have. If it the first time the company has briefed you, just say:

> Since this is our first briefing I would like a high-level overview of the company and your products. What problem do you solve? Who are the key members of the team and their backgrounds? What is your funding level, and who are your investors? How are you going to market (channel versus direct mix)? What is your regional coverage so far? How do you differentiate in the market? And anything you can share about customer wins and partnerships.

When you are engaged in researching a particular topic you can provide more specific questions.

The vendor will probably use a standard slide presentation to brief you. Ask for a hard copy so you don't have to take screen shots. After your 100th briefing you will become impatient with the "set up" where they show you just how important the problem they address is. Don't feel bad about politely interrupting and asking them to skip ahead to the product slides. I have heard analysts say: "I am willing to stipulate the problem and the market need, so let's jump to your solution." If the people briefing you are inexperienced or just bad at their job, they may launch into a sales pitch. You can cut them short by challenging their claims. I recently had a large vendor, owned by private equity, meaning they do not report sales numbers, claim they were growing faster than industry CAGR. That was such an outrageous, unsubstantiated claim, I had to stop the product manager. You too will grow to hate such claims. You are the industry analyst, so you must determine the veracity of those claims. Does the vendor claim they grew 200% year over year? How do they explain that while LinkedIn reports they dropped 6% in employment over the same period?

Keep in mind that your one goal during a briefing is to demonstrate that you understand their space. I love it when the team on the call slowly begins to understand that this is not a call with a journalist that their PR person set up because you write for a trade publication or Forbes.com. By my questions and suggestions they figure out that I understand their industry, what they do, and what challenges they face. I never do a sales pitch on a briefing. At most, if they ask how to work more closely with me I will run through the things I have done for other vendors: white papers, speaking events, webinars, and strategy sessions. But always keep it low key so you do not break the barrier of vendor-analyst separation.

That said, once the team realizes how smart you are, you will be on their radar. They will pay attention to your research. They may even reach out to ask you to provide a quote for a press release and ask that you serve as press reference. Then they introduce you to journalists who are writing about them. You cannot endorse the product but you can validate their claims for the market or the need for their products.

If they inspire you with some observation, go ahead and write about it and link to their website. Never for pay! As a matter of fact, if they have retained you for any work you probably won't write about them because you would have to disclose that relationship.

Take notes during the briefing. Write down every number they claim: Number of customers, number of employees, number of partners. The next time they brief you, ask about those numbers. Knowing these things helps you gauge the growth/success of the company. Besides, if you don't take notes, and don't have an eidetic memory, you are going to forget everything about them. Even if you are not working on a research note about their space, imagine that someday you will and will have to write two or three hundred words about the company. Jot that down right after the call or at the end of the day.

Another aspect of keeping notes is to call a vendor out when they are lying. It should be no surprise that they do. A journalist will repeat verbatim what a vendor tells them. An analyst needs corroborating evidence.

When I was at Gartner and helping to cover the Managed Security Service Provider space I had multiple calls with a large MSSP in Atlanta, Georgia. I knew the founders and the PR guy had worked for Netrex, the first company I worked for in the cybersecurity space. The key metric in the MSSP space was how many devices did they manage. On the first call this guy said 1,500, which would have made them the biggest in the space back in 2001. Six month later, that PR guy had moved on and the new PR guy, not knowing what his predecessor had said, claimed 1,100 devices under management. A year later I was getting briefed by the CTO of another MSSP in Boston. He had recently joined after leaving the company in Atlanta, so I asked him how many devices the Atlanta company had had under management. He said "never more than 500." Vendors should never lie to analysts. A good analyst will uncover the truth eventually.

There was another company in Boston that sold DDoS defense appliances. Every year they would report to Gartner their revenue, which was calculated by multiplying devices shipped by their list prices. Of course they had significant discounts for volume sales, not to mention the points they gave to distributors and resellers, so their reported revenue was probably 50% higher than actual revenue.

The vendor briefings are your best opportunity to establish a connection with the founders and executives of the companies that make up your industry. Make good use of them.

Conferences

Conferences are another good venue for making connections. As an industry analyst, you will often be able to get a media pass. Do the conference a favor and actually write about the event and your impressions. It is only fair, considering they gave you a free pass. When you have down time, hang out in the media center. You will see many of your journalist and analyst friends there. The conversations about what is hot and what is passé may spark some ideas.

Besides, you rarely get to interact with the other thought leaders in your space so this is your chance.

If you are listed as a media person, you will get many requests for briefings during the conference. Take a notebook then write down your impressions at the end of the day.

Spend as much time as you can on the show floor. Search out the booths of vendors you have not seen before. Often the founders will be doing booth duty. Share your wisdom with them and get their cards. Connect with them on LinkedIn later to request a formal briefing.

Wander past the big vendors and your clients to show your face, just as a reminder of your presence in the industry. Take note of which booths have the CEOs in them. In my space you used to be able to find the founders and CEOs of even the biggest companies doing booth duty. Now they seem to be more comfortable hanging out in a hotel suite and taking appointments. I still count CEO sightings on the show floor.

Beware the party circuit in the evenings. Definitely sign up for all the invitations you get. Perhaps drop by the parties of your clients. Your presence, as an industry thought leader, is a compliment to them. But watch the intake of free drinks, you have to be up and raring to go the next morning. That said, there is nothing like a drunk salesperson to tell you what is really going on at their company.

Speaking gigs

The secret to a successful speaking event is preparation and practice. As you assemble your slides, think about how you are going to weave them into a story. Practice your pitch standing up. Think about your stance, your hand motions, any props you may use. Practice the transitions between slides. When you know which slide comes next and how you are going to introduce it, you know you are ready. Figure out how to inject excitement and energy into your talk. As painful as it may be to watch, record yourself delivering your pitch, and be analytical in your self-critique. Run over your slides the night before and the morning of. Make sure the AV people have your slides and they were not corrupted in transmission. Carry a PDF and PowerPoint backup on a USB device.

Sometimes you will be on a tight schedule, breezing in an hour before your time slot and rushing out afterwards. You may be doing a double header—two paid engagements in the same day. Or you may have to catch a flight to the next engagement. After a week like that your head will be spinning.

But, typically you will give more time to your client. They may ask you to attend the VIP dinner the night before, or meet with press or customers before your keynote. I always do this gladly. It presents more opportunities to learn and connect.

You can judge the success of your presentation by audience engagement, the questions they ask, how many people come up afterwards to say how much they enjoyed it. Sometimes it does not go well. The most brutal question I ever got was, "So, what is your point?" Soul crushing. The best indication that your pitch went well is that the client engages you for more presentations.

Analyst Days

Many large vendors hold an annual Analyst Day. They invite the key analysts from Gartner, Forrester, Ovum, IDC, and maybe a few respected independent analysts like you. The vendor pays for accommodations and travel. These are well worth your time. In addition to the deep dive into the vendor's business, you get to see how each executive performs in a high intensity environment. The audience knows their business and their competitors, and they do not hesitate to ask tough questions.

The other benefit is you get to mix with your peers, people who have the same job as you and think about the same things.

Speed Dating Events

Some PR firms and event companies organize speed dating events. They pay for the analysts to come for a day of one-on-one meetings with a dozen vendors, and the vendors pay a fee for participating. You usually spend 30 minutes sitting at a small table with a couple of people from each vendor. It is a great way to get a lot of briefings done in a short period. Once again, you get to mix with your peers the night before, over coffee, and lunch. You may see your counterparts at the other firms only once a year at events like these, but over time they become your friends.

Investor calls

It's fun to join the quarterly earnings calls for the publicly traded vendors you cover. Sign up for a free account at seekingalpha.com, the stock trading site, and create a list of companies you follow. You will get notified when they schedule earnings call for each quarter, along with instructions for dialing in. At the end of the CEO's and CFO's presentation, the operator will ask for questions. Get ready to press the right button to be put in the queue. State your name and organization and your question. In this way you will get on the radar of the executives and the investor relations person. Even the other participants, who are rarely industry analysts but are stock analysts, may take note of you.

They may reach out later to see if they can engage you. I have found that stock analysts as a rule are almost single-mindedly focused on guessing what the next quarter's earnings per share will be. Even if they appear interested in strategic positioning, they are still only interested in how much a strategy will cost and will it increase or decrease quarterly earnings. Your cogent questions will stick out. Even if you don't participate, the investor relations person will know that you were on the call because you had to identify yourself when you called in.

Talking to press

Throughout your day you have to make yourself available to journalists that are looking for insights into your industry. I find there are two types of calls with journalists. Most often they have a theme in mind for an article that their editor assigned and they are looking for pithy quotes from independent experts in the field. You will probably already know about the event they are calling to write about, such as an acquisition, a breach, or a government action. So have your analogies ready.

The other type of call is exploratory. You spend up to half an hour educating the journalist about what makes the industry tick. Those can be frustrating because sometimes you do not even get quoted in the piece. But you have established yourself with the journalist as an expert and they are sure to reach out again.

The daily flow of communication

In any given day you will be answering emails or LinkedIn messages from folks. It could be a founder asking for advice on an investor pitch or considering a pivot in their product strategy. Or it could be coordinating emails from a marketing team for your upcoming webinar. There will be a constant barrage of PR people offering their latest take on news events, or asking for briefings around a funding event or a new study their client is going to publish. Often you will be given a heads up on news under embargo. Respect the embargo if you do write or tweet about the news. Always be nice to PR people.

You will also be contacted by executives you have worked with in the past who are looking for a job. Help them out if you can. I often hear from salespeople who want to know about the advisability of joining a certain company. I always give them my two cents. When headhunters reach out, let them know that so-and-so is available.

A word on headhunters. Many will offer a finder's fee if you suggest someone they place, but I have never collected such a fee. I have learned it is just not worth it to have a relationship with a headhunter. The greatest value is the connection you have created when you hook somebody up.

This is the life of an analyst. Being busy equates to success. It means you are getting the word out and building relationships. At the end of the year you will be amazed at how well you did, and chagrined at the tax bill you owe to the government if you run your own firm. Beware of something I have had to learn repeatedly: when you get busy working on client engagements, you slack off on writing and publishing. If you experience a lull in business, immediately start blogging and writing again. That always has an immediate impact and generates new activity, which leads to new paying gigs.

Another compelling aspect of the analyst life is the ability to work from anywhere. Take advantage of the summer lull to schedule an extended stay someplace nice. But it also has to have a comfortable place to write and take calls. Check the internet connectivity before you book. For you it may be a cruise or a trip to a tropical paradise. Unlike other small businesses, that never release you from the day to day grind, being an industry analyst provides a comfortable lifestyle.

Moving On or Growing Up

Sometimes being an industry analyst is just a stop along the way in a successful career. As an analyst you are exposed to lots of opportunities and you are constantly building your reputation. By the time you are being quoted in the mainstream press and doing regular commentary on television, you will find that offers of employment come your way. As I stated before, this is the greatest risk to your life as an independent analyst. It can be difficult getting established and the more time you spend alone with the burden of generating income with your writing and research, the more attractive a salary job looks.

Your spouse may love the idea of a steady income too, one that pays health insurance and disability insurance. It's hard to think about, but what if you get sick or have an accident that impairs your ability to type or work long hours? Definitely look into disability insurance.

I have been wooed away from the analyst business three times. The first time I left Gartner to join Webroot Software. One thing I have learned is that being an analyst at heart makes it difficult to fit in at a large company. It may take up to six months to figure out that the company is heading in the wrong direction. Besides, you miss the independence. Webroot was a high flying company in the anti-spyware business. The strategy was to use its foothold in the consumer space to break into the enterprise space. Unfortunately, soon after Webroot introduced its enterprise product, McAfee announced they were going to add signatures to its ePO product to detect and block "potentially unwanted software." When your product is turned into a feature of the established vendors' products you are going to have trouble. For the 15 months I was at Webroot, not once was I asked by the CEO or board for my input on strategy. Yet every week CEOs of other startups would call asking for advice on their strategies. I missed that analyst advisory role. When I finally realized that Webroot was never going public, I gave my two weeks' notice.

Webroot was very helpful in my transition to becoming an independent analyst. They transferred my blog domain, threatchaos.com, to me and there were no hard feelings.

Only two years later I was at a crisis point for IT-Harvest, the firm I launched after leaving Webroot. (Note that Gartner enforces a 12 month non-compete on its analysts, something they instituted early on after a group of analysts in Australia quit together to create a competitor to Gartner.) I had paying customers in 2006 but revenue was lumpy, some months would be great, with $20-50k in revenue, some months zero. I had just written an open letter to Check Point Software that appeared in *Network World* magazine. That article spurred Ken Xie, the founder of Fortinet, to call and ask me to join as Chief Marketing Officer.

In November of 2006 I joined Fortinet. I was the highest paid executive and I had enough options to make me rich when the company went public. Unfortunately, I still had the entrepreneurial bug and after a year started to make plans to launch a managed security service provider using Fortinet's security appliances. Fortinet was supportive of my plans but understandably did not want me doing that while on their payroll, so I left.

The MSSP did not work out at all so in the fall of 2008 I fell back on IT-Harvest and relaunched the independent analyst business just as the global financial crisis began. 2009 was a rough year, but if a startup can survive a recession it is usually in good shape during the recovery, and business grew steadily.

By 2016 business was great, so great that I had a horrific debt to the IRS. The lumpiness of the analyst business makes it hard to pay estimated taxes every quarter. It's the end of the quarter and you owe $20k that you do not have to the IRS, so an offer to join Blancco as Chief Strategy Officer was enticing. A client CEO that I had a lot of respect for had been appointed CEO of AIM-listed Blancco Technology Group. The idea of being part of a functional management team was appealing. Soon after joining though it became apparent that the promised "fun" was not there. The company did not have the resources to afford a highly paid evangelist. So, on my advice, they let me go in the fall of 2017.

Back to IT-Harvest. It is much better, I learned, to launch a company at the end of a ten-year business cycle than at the beginning. After three years I can say it is possible to build a successful analyst firm. Once you get your head above water, solve the unevenness in revenue with the right product mix, and build the freedom to try new things, you are in good shape. Perhaps good enough to weather a global pandemic.

Based on my experience, here are the reasons to move on from being an analyst:
- You are not cut out for the uncertainty in income. If you do not have a high risk tolerance, you may find being in business for yourself too stressful. It is reassuring to look at your accounts receivable. At least you can plan on that income in the next month or so. But what about when you have zero outstanding invoices? That means you have to get a client, do the work, invoice, and wait for them to pay. It is hard to focus on your long term projects like a book or a new research note when you have to do something today to get money in the door.
- You get an opportunity that is (1) a step up in your career, such as a C level role at a successful company, and (2) extends your impact in your industry. Alternatively, you may be recruited to lead an analyst practice at a big firm. This could be the best of both worlds. These are so tempting.
- You like working in large organizations, even with the frustrations and politics that come with that. Perhaps you should look to joining a large analyst firm. Leverage your experience as an independent to get that job.
- You actually like commuting to work. I have heard people say they enjoy driving to work. It gives them time to prepare and get into the work day. And they get to decompress on the way home.

And here is why you should tough out the hard times and stick to the industry analyst business:
- You enjoy being master of your own fate. An analyst does not do well with authority, especially the silly things required of an employee. Time sheets? Expense reports? Employee evaluations? All-hands meetings? No thanks.
- You tend to make a bad employee. Some people are just not meant to work in a big organization. That's OK.
- You can't stand the thought of commuting to work. Two or three times a year I find myself driving during rush hour. I cannot begin to think about doing that every day. I much prefer the 75 feet I walk to my writing shed every morning. Besides, what a waste of time and gasoline.
- You get multiple requests to drop everything to join a company. This would be a great indication that you are on the cusp of succeeding as an independent analyst. You have made a name for yourself. Multiple CEOs are so impressed with your work that they want you to work for them. Resist!

Moving On or Growing Up

- You have customers that value your help. There is nothing more satisfying than happy customers. Key indicator that they are happy: they keep coming back to you.

There are other ways to stay in business while getting some stability of having employment. One is to get a job as a teacher. If you have a PhD you can become a professor. In my experience. professors tend not to be bound by conflicts of interest. Often they are encouraged to make money on the side consulting. You should be able to ground yourself with a professor role while continuing to be an industry analyst. If you do not have a PhD, an adjunct professor role might open up.

Not strictly a separate job is the arena of advisory boards and board of director roles.

Advisory boards

Despite the danger of presenting a conflict of interest it is extremely valuable to be on an advisory board. The typical arrangement is that you get a small percentage of the company's stock in exchange for your participation in quarterly meetings. These meetings, usually remote, are a great way to learn about what the company is experiencing and to interact with the other advisory board members. Your bio appears on the company website. Occasionally the CEO will call with some immediate question.

Board of Director roles

Being on the actual board of a company is completely different than participating in an advisory role. As a board member, you have fiduciary responsibility for the company's actions. You vote on key decisions such as funding. You will be involved in firing and hiring the CEO. You will also get a complete window into the company operations. This is invaluable experience and fodder for your analyst mind. Board meetings are in person so you have to travel once a quarter, but you usually are well fed and your expenses are reimbursed.

Most venture-funded firms do not pay board members, but larger companies do. There are many people who are professional board members in semi-retirement. It can be very lucrative.

Anytime you are listed on a company's website as a contributor you have to be hyper aware of the conflict of interest you are creating. You are supposed to be objective and independent. If you have stock options in a key player in your space, how can you expect to get work from its competitors? You probably cannot. So look for board opportunities outside your primary space.

Growing the Business

Being a sole proprietor is always a risk. Every dollar earned comes from the work you do yourself. But you have flexibility to move that work into the areas you enjoy the most. You can even slow down if you are burning out. But most often you will want to continue to grow your business. I am still working on a model to do that.

Create a repeatable business, something that you know works. Things like:

Video production. Six months before the biggest conference in your industry, let all the vendors know that you are going to be conducting video interviews during the conference. This is a chance for the vendor to engage you for far less than your daily rate. Schedule interviews back-to-back every hour during the first couple days of the conference. Hire a local camera crew. Reserve a large suite that has room to set up a studio. The first time we did this for IT-Harvest, the crew showed up the night before and draped the backdrops and set up their cameras. Over the next three days, we did 30 interviews.

The first year you do this, plan for one day of interviews. Extend that after you get ten people signed up. If you get efficient at capturing good interviews, you can schedule them even 45 minutes. Mind you, it is physically exhausting to do that many interviews, but do the math: it's a good business.

The format is simple. It's an interview with the analyst so after introducing the guest, ask, "What does your company do? What problem do you solve? How is your product sold? Deployed? Installed? What's next for your company?" Simple.

Post production of videos requires help. You have professional raw video, but you need an intro, outro, and titles. Find somebody willing to do that for 10% of what you charge the customer.

Professionally produced video typically costs $1,000/minute so if you charge less than $15,000 for a 15 minute final cut, you are offering a good value. Let the vendor use the footage however they want to.

Think about this: the vendors are paying you to create a video that they are going to promote on their websites and on social media, which means they are actually promoting you!

A complete listing of all the vendors in your space broken down by subcategory and region. This is something that once created can be updated continuously. You can write about each category and include the list, with links to each vendor website. You can publish the directory, as I do in the *Security Yearbook*. A published directory begs the question: why not sell advertising? Do it. Update the list every year. You could even sell a subscription to your directory and provide continuous updates. There is tremendous value in curating all that data. You use it in your own research and you generate revenue from others that need access to it.

Look into the opportunities to speak at sales kickoff (SKO) meetings and partner events. Most vendors begin every fiscal year with an SKO in the first two weeks, often in nice locations. Reach out and suggest that they hire the industry expert to come in and provide their thoughts on where the industry is going. January is the primary month for these events, but July is the second most frequent beginning to a fiscal year. Lining up work in July can do a lot to iron out the seasonality in your business.

Partner events are even more lavish than SKOs. The vendor brings its resellers in from all over the world. They are usually held at a resort or even on a cruise ship. They are a great speaking opportunity for an industry expert.

Thick Skin

Being an analyst requires thick skin. When you start out, it can be devastating to be derided for your writing by people in the industry that you respect. You may have said that their products are not worth spending money on. You may have said a competing technology spells the end of life for the incumbent. The vitriol is often in proportion to the amount of influence you have in the industry. Over time, you learn some lessons. First, strong responses mean you are on the right path. Those tearing you down will be very public. But even during the most violent attacks, you will get support via back channels from people who agree with you but never felt they had the platform to come out and make the same claims. They will thank you for taking a stance. In my own experience, it may take me several years to come to a conclusion about a direction the industry is taking. I shy away from making the bold proclamations because I know what the pushback will be like. Billionaires saying you don't know what you are talking about. Journalists mischaracterizing your statements. Thousands of comments and tweets that you are tempted to respond to, as you read every one of them.

Focus on the supportive statements you get both in public and through those back channels. Read the formal responses, and compare your thesis to their arguments. Does it still hold? Did you miss something? Do you need to change your stance? If years later it turns out you were completely wrong, don't worry, just say so. Remember you have to be wrong some percentage of the time. Just be transparent. Your mea culpa may be more popular than your original prediction.

The FW MQ story

What follows is an excerpt from *UP and to the RIGHT*. It relates my first experience in the limelight as a disruptive industry analyst.

Let me tell the story of the North American Enterprise Firewall Magic Quadrant during my stint at Gartner from 2000 to 2004. Keep in mind that in those earlier days, Gartner had not refined its MQ methodology, it *was* more subjective than objective.

I was the third analyst to take on the Firewall MQ. I inherited an MQ that had mostly legacy vendors in it: Check Point, Cisco, Gauntlet, even Sidewinder and Raptor. It had been several years since there were any major moves of any of the dots. I came at the MQ from a fresh perspective and hoped to use the MQ to drive the vendors towards what I saw happening in the market.

Gartner's strength and market advantage in the research industry is its large client base. Today it has over 11,000 customers, mostly large enterprises, state and local governments, universities, and financial services firms. Gartner analysts derive their expertise from the continual interaction with the IT departments of these organizations. I remember thinking when I first joined Gartner that I may not have been an "expert" on the IT security industry when they hired me, but after six months of four to eight calls every single working day with CIOs and their teams, I *became* an expert. The questions posed in these "inquiries" from clients were often the same and could quickly be used to identify common concerns, popular trends in vendor selection, and an increasing level of interest in my particular area: network security.

At one point, a vendor that had gone to market in the heady days of the Internet boom as a roll-up of security companies (Network Associates, Inc.) arranged to have a massive strategic engagement session with eight separate analysts. This was very unusual and very expensive—about $80k to get all the analysts to fly out to California to meet with the entire executive team led by Gene Hodges, president of NAI. It was a day-long review of each of the markets NAI played in. Years before, NAI had acquired the Gauntlet firewall and it was the basis of their network security solution. There was just one problem: Over the previous year, out of several hundred inquiries about firewalls, just two were about Gauntlet. When it came time for me to present, I flatly told the executive team it was time to "End of Life" the Gauntlet firewall. It did not have any market traction with the large enterprises that NAI was targeting and that comprised Gartner's customer base.

As I made my statement, backed up by my mentor, dialed in on the squawk box in the center of the long conference table, I looked around the room to judge the reaction. I saw heads nodding and eye contact being made. I knew that our advice was right on target and we were confirming a decision already contemplated by the executive team. What occurred next is a lesson in what happens when an analyst makes a bold call. The repercussions can impact the analyst's career and bring out the worst in a vendor.

When I drafted the next version of the Firewall Magic Quadrant, I removed Gauntlet altogether. Keep in mind that Gauntlet had been carried over as a Leader and now I was erasing it. When I sent out the draft to all the vendors listed in the MQ I started to receive urgent calls from the Gartner inquiry desk. The VP of marketing for NAI needed to talk to me. He was traveling in Europe but would make the time. When we connected, he was livid. "Not only are we the most visionary firewall vendor but we have the best ability to execute!" he shouted. These qualities, of course, are the two axes of the MQ. I told him that he should check with his executive team because perhaps I was privy to upper management sentiments that he was not. The next call I got was from one of the most senior analysts at Gartner. Ken McGee was old-school and had been with Gartner from the early days when everyone worked in the small building at the end of Top Gallant Road in Stamford, Connecticut, and Gideon Gartner was still at the helm. During my four-day Gartner Boot Camp training, Ken had come in to present on "Being a Curmudgeon." This was the first time I had ever taken a call from him. He wanted to say that the marketing guy from NAI was raising hell and wanted me fired. I explained the sequence of events and all he said was, "Check your facts and stick to your guns. We will support you all the way."

I published the MQ without Gauntlet and two months later NAI announced the End of Life (EOL) of Gauntlet and passed the product off to Secure Computing, another vendor of firewalls. In a still-unexplained twist of events, NAI, now McAfee, acquired Secure Computing in 2008 before being acquired in turn by Intel in 2010.

Gartner analysts have to deal with irate marketing people all the time. It is a symptom of bad analyst relations (AR) and the frustration many vendors experience when dealing with Gartner.

It helps to have a large organization behind you when you make disruptive calls. You are sheltered from defamation law suits, vendors with a larger media presence than you will ever have, and there is little risk of it impacting your livelihood. As an independent analyst you may have to tread more lightly.

That said, the worst thing I have experienced criticizing a large vendor is for them to blacklist me. And frankly, that would be good advice to any vendor that objects to an independent analyst's take. Just ignore them. Pushing back could just serve to draw more attention to the criticism, especially from the trade press, which loves a controversy.

So, be cautious in the battles you choose and stick to your guns when you do choose a battle. Learn to cope with the negative backlash by seeking out and relishing the positive responses.

Analyst Contributions

Tom Austin Interview

Tom Austin was one of the most senior analysts at Gartner when I joined in 2000. He spent a total of 26 years at Gartner building the practice and sharing his insights to a worldwide audience. After retiring he brought together The Analyst Syndicate, a group of 24 independent industry analysts.

How did you become an industry analyst?

Born in '49, I was a child of the '50s: tubes or valves and then transistors fascinated me. Sputnik 1 and 2 thrilled and worried me. Echo 1 stands out in memory, as do all the rocket launches, from Wolfe's pantheon in "The Right Stuff" all the way to the Apollo capsule ground fire that killed Grissom and two other astronauts. By then, I was in college...

I loved following stories on emerging technologies in *Scientific American*, *Popular Science*, and other publications in the '60s. A lot of it was probably fiction but it didn't matter. I absorbed it all. By the '70s, I was deep into computers, system architectures, and core technologies.

I'd learned a bit of computer programming (Fortran II) as an undergrad at Georgetown in the '60s, an early IBM 360 system. I played with programming on an Olivetti Programma 101 in 1970. By '71, I was off in grad school (Brain Sciences) and using primitive minicomputers of the day (Modcomp, HP, Data General, etc.) for real-time process control and data collection in the lab. I taught myself machine language programming and modified the OS on one of the systems to make it do more of what I needed. Who knew you weren't supposed to do that?

By fall 1975 I was off teaching Psych in a tenure-track position at a small, liberal arts college. I soon decided I did not want to take a post-doc to finish my PhD and compete all over again for a good starter tenure-track position.

While teaching college, I dug into their new Digital Equipment PDP 11/40 RSTS time sharing system; learned all about system programming on that machine; and created Computer Managed Instruction software.

Armed with that, as well as real-time systems work, I bolted to a job in the computer industry in November 1976. At Digital Equipment Corp. (DEC) in Washington, I signed on as an SE (software specialist in their terminology), supporting customers and sales of RSTS-based systems and went off and learned the internals of RSX-11M. In 11 months, I moved to a management position in field software services and started to think about moving to a marketing or engineering position in headquarters (the greater "Maynard MA area").

Three short years later, I was a marketing manager at DEC in Lab Data Products (LDP) product line in Marlboro, MA, and the art of being an industry analyst (as well as business plan designer, communications specialist, negotiator, and inventory allocator) were all part of my job description.

I came across a very early, quite-voluminous paper on "Office Automation" or something similar in the early '80s, written by Gideon Gartner and one other person. I was inspired by it at the time. Little would I know how Gartner would influence me later.

In 1982, I was running a task force charged with coming up with a recommendation on how to undercut UNIX, which senior executives were convinced was eating DEC's business. We came up with a proposal we thought was brilliant: Give away VMS (DEC's 32-bit virtual OS) and allow others to port it to run on other hardware platforms, effectively undercutting UNIX's competitive advantages against DEC. This was one of my great personal disappointments. We got laughed out of the meeting when we presented it. We were right, but DEC wouldn't hear of it. This inspired me later in my career...

By fall 1983, after the being passed over for a job as engineering manager for the Lab Data Products group, I moved to the technical OEM product line where I created at least two breakthrough marketing programs: one, the creation of communities of CEOs of tech startups meeting monthly to identify issues and strategies for dealing with them (Santa Clara, CA, and Boston, MA, later followed with several other cities) and the other, working with the early-stage incubators of the day, exemplified by the MIT Enterprise Forum (and affiliated programs in places like Cal Tech), serving as judges and advisors in their monthly business-plan competitions. We got a lot of exposure to startups, angel, and venture investors.

In the fall of '86, I moved to DEC's Office Information Systems product group to take over product marketing responsibility for the "ALL-IN-1" products. By early '87, Gartner was trying to hire me to cover Office Information Systems for them but I couldn't imagine forcing my family to move from New Hampshire to Stamford, CT, so I recommended someone else at Digital who they hired for that job.

Lots of other interesting events followed, including negotiating the acquisition of another firm (which took five tries before the executive committee agreed), but it was pretty clear, by 1992-93, it was over for DEC.

Enter Gartner for a second time. By the end of 1993, I had agreed to join Gartner (without moving to Connecticut) and spent nearly 25 great years there doing many interesting things. I'll write that some other time.

What do you think makes a good industry analyst? What traits, habits, background?

Great industry analysts possess an insatiable thirst to know the unknowable, to try to predict the future, to be willing to second guess everyone (including themselves), to buck conventional wisdom, to make mistakes and learn from them.

They also need to have excellent communication skills, marketing savvy, and a sense for finding the unknown—including the unknown unknowns.

Great analysts reinvent themselves, extract common sense across their experiences, and refine the specific gems they find along the way.

Great analysts create primarily through synthesis. Synthesis is an important habit. To do it right requires listening, sensing, feeling, and walking in the other party's shoes, asking a few questions when necessary, reading, and writing.

Writing is a critical synthesis tool. We learn by listening and by reading. Some of the learning comes from reading what we've written to discover meaning hidden even from us. And more learning will come from testing what we've learned from our reading (and sensing and so forth).

Great analysts take risks. Not too crazy. They need to be right a little more often than wrong. Analysts who are always right aren't bold enough, or they have memory deficiencies, or they're trying to deceive themselves or others.

Good analysts? They're absolutely needed, too!

How do you identify a good research area?
We thrive on uncertainty. Our buyers and readers and sellers need to know the sharp edges, the analysis that leads to us identifying those edges, and the advice we offer to deal with those sharp edges. The uncertainties (sharp edges and all) can be of many types: technological, social, economic, regulatory, and so on.

Some customers and readers want to hear "don't worry, nothing happening here, move on." That can be a bad research area. Or it can serve as a foundation that proves you're not running around with your air on fire everywhere and you're selective in terms of the places where you're seeking customer-prospect-market attention.

Is it possible to pivot to other research areas?
Totally! Pivot to adjacencies if they're fertile. Or slowly build competencies in a new area and then unmask them in a bold pivot. The original Evel Knievel never did successfully jump the Grand Canyon. Plan your jumps wisely. Test them tentatively. Work up to the big one.

Is the life of an industry analyst a good one?
Keeps the brain active, your belly and passport full. And you can also make a good living at it. (Just be honest, don't break any laws like US insider trading regulations, and treat everyone fairly.)

What was the high point of your analyst career? Low point?
High points:
- Growing The Analyst Syndicate
- Watching great Maverick research emerge from Gartner
- Getting boo-ed on stage predicting the rise of Consumerization of Technology, ca. 2003

Low points:
- Almost leaving Gartner to take a CTO job in 1999 (bored with covering Office and Network Computing)
- Spending January 2000-early 2004 outside of an Analyst role (Research Mgmt. at Gartner)

What follows is the email Tom Austin sent to the research community within Gartner when he retired.

Analyst Contributions

From: Austin, Tom
Sent: Wednesday, June 27, 2018 6:21 AM
Subject: It's been a great run...

I turn 70 in March. I've spent almost 25 years, more than half my adult life, here at Gartner! What a fantastic journey! I love you all, everyone inside and out. The intellectual processes and products. The personal friendships. The vigor and intensity. The opportunity to learn from you and to help. The Maverick Program (est. 2005) still delivers disruptive innovation with explosions of creativity in almost every corner of what we do.

This is a Jimmy Stewart moment, from *It's A Wonderful Life*. To many, that's a Christmas romantic drama-comedy. To Stewart, it was a moment of crisis in his personal life, as he came back from fighting in World War 2, afraid he couldn't reestablish himself as an actor. Stress and PTSD led to his grounding as a B24 pilot. The suicide attempt in the movie could easily have been about acting. He reinvented himself and made it. Reinvention should be the center of all our lives.

I can't say enough about how I have valued the opportunity to reinvent myself here, numerous times. Take the initiative. Just do it. Force yourself. Look at the output of the Maverick Program to get insights to consider. (It's a pity we don't invest more in that great program.) Life is too short to cover just one area here. Organizational processes will focus you on what you know now and do now. But you're more than that, better than that. You can be many great things. Believe it. Do them all with personal passion. Accept the risk and fear of moving into a new area. Be great at it even if your knees shake from time to time.

Reinvent yourself. I repeatedly reinvented myself here through all of you, both 1:1 and in larger communities. Innovating in communities is a core strength. Don't lose it. Don't rely on formal communities.

Creativity at scale has always struck me as a virtual oxymoron. We don't make cars or boxes of cereal. We are merchants of insight and advice. In this business, we have to focus on the intangibles that make Gartner great rather than the simple tangible metrics that are so much easier to find. Huawei cranks out products efficiently while Apple achieved greatness by a focus on unique value and identity. That's why Apple is the true price leader in segment. They maximize productivity via great products sold at the highest price (with low cost assembly). Apple will fall from grace if they become too formulaic and predictable. Us too. (I silently fear for both.)

Take the untaken path. Thought leadership comes from hard work and open ears. Clients (both users and vendors) have provided the crucible through which everything I've done has been shaped and reshaped over the years. Take away something from every interaction you have. I love (and will greatly miss) the Summits and Symposia because I would take away at least one great client insight—from the client to us—that would then get worked into the script and eventually into presentations and then the written research months (or years) later. Great ideas don't flow from the head of Zeus. Test ideas with clients. Feel their emotions. Practice the spiel constantly, sensing out new or alternate angles and points of view. Get out of your and their comfort zones.

Hype is seductive. Don't be seduced. Politely question the BS that vendors weave into visions our clients adopt (and the press repeats). We don't (and shouldn't) bash vendors for that action (it's a tragedy of the commons thing) but we can conceptually warn our clients about the biggest whoppers out there. Ideas, not companies or people. And the clients will get it.

Live life with passion. Invest yourself in your family and friends outside of Gartner. We only live so long (and have no idea how long that will be), but the nearest and dearest aren't here at work. I'll miss Gartner but look forward to spending more time with family and reinventing myself yet again!

At a personal level...goodbye until we meet again. (My last day here is 30 June.) Stay in touch when it strikes your fancy, days, months, years from now. (I might even start a blog or three at tom-austin.com about some of my many passions. All in due course.)

Jon Oltsik Interview

Jon Oltsik began his analyst career at Forrester. After a stint back in industry he helped form Enterprise Strategy Group and is Senior Principal Analyst there. He blogs at CSO Online.

In 1995 I was not happy at EMC, which had acquired Epoch Systems. They were very hardware oriented, and I was from a software company. So, I started exploring options, and I was interviewed by the Aberdeen group. I had no idea what an industry analyst did but, in exploring that opportunity, I felt like it really worked to my strengths, and it would help me improve some of my weaknesses. I also thought it was a good place to network, to learn the industry, and to get connected to people. I thought, "Yeah, this could be a cool job."

I got a job offer there. It didn't work out, but soon after I interviewed and got a job offer at Forrester in '95, which I accepted and stayed until '99. Forrester had five or six practice areas back then, probably in the range of 30-40 analysts. Then, I went back into the market during the internet boom.

When things kind of died after the internet boom, I found myself doing some things on my own. And then I joined ESG (Enterprise Strategy Group) in 2003.

There are several things that contribute to being a good industry analyst. First, you have to be a subject matter expert. And that means understanding the technology that you're covering; understanding it from the user perspective, not the technology perspective, not the industry perspective, although those are important, too. But in my view, it's how are users consuming this technology? Why do they need it? What are the requirements? What do they get out of it? If you know that, you're well along the way, and you can then understand or at least communicate that to customers, whether those customers are other end users or vendors.

Now, you have to be able to communicate all this effectively. You have to be a reasonably good speaker, a reasonably good writer, and be reasonably good at communicating complex topics into bite-size chunks. You have to be productive because the job involves a lot of writing, a lot of phone calls. I think your interpersonal skills are important for success. You don't have to be the most charismatic or the best communicator, but I think those are important. You can't be bad at either of those and be a successful analyst.

I think the user perspective is important, but it is also important to understand other roles within the organization. More and more we're talking to different roles within vendors. For example, we're talking to lead generation people, and marketing programs people. So, it's good to have an understanding of what they do, too. But at the end of the day, what our job is, in my view, is to understand how users or how and why users are using certain technologies, and then be able to write and communicate about that.

An industry analyst job is a good transformational job. If you're a user, you may want to get on the vendor side, or if you're a user and you've been working with particular vendors, and you want to broaden your experience, it could help. Depending on where you work, you can really broaden your knowledge base becoming an analyst because you do have access to a lot of really smart people who want to talk to you.

To pick an industry to cover you could look at where the investment is going. You could talk to startups who've just recently been funded along the same theme.

But I do think it's important to determine what you're interested in. What's fascinating to you? What do you love to read about? What do you love to study? What do you love to talk to people about? If you have that passion and you can develop that understanding, then I think you can be successful. There are plenty of opportunities for an analyst because, again, you get to talk to people, and you get access to possibly new information under NDA. People come to you and ask you for your ideas. You can develop your skills, or you can develop your knowledge around a certain topic, but the topic has to be something you're really interested in.

The good thing of course with technology is it's always changing. Things that were once old become new again, sort of like next generation firewalls, or next generation AV. So, if you can focus in a particular area, you should be good, at least in security, for now.

The more esoteric, the more developing, the more immature a market is, the more you have to have an angle. You do have to do your homework, and find a particular segment or niche that is expanding, where there's money or where people are making bets on investments, and there's just a lot of guessing. If you can fill those gaps with knowledge, then I think there's a market. But you do have to pick and choose because some markets will be too nascent for that type of coverage. Some will burn out over time.

Is it a good career? It's a good one for the right person. So for instance, I've worked with really smart people who don't write well. And it's been a struggle for them. I've worked with really charismatic people who are really good on their feet, but weren't good at doing the homework and backing up their bravado with facts and research. So, it's not for everyone. But if you do like technology, if you like to write and speak, and you're willing to do the work, then I think it's a really good job.

The high point of being an analyst for me is when you feel accomplished in a particular area, and you've written about it, and gotten accolades for your coverage and for your thoughts, and the phone starts to ring, and people come to you. Those are the rewarding moments.

One of the occupational hazards of the analyst community is there are a lot of bullshitters in the market. And I kind of hinted at this before, but I think those people flame out. It can be really impactful for a short amount of time before people see through their act, and the second or third time you meet that person, they're saying the same things they said the first time.

There's a certain amount of diligence and persistence involved, but if you can do that, and you're passionate about the topics, you're willing to put in the work to learn something, and then you can figure out the angles on it, I think that's very rewarding.

On the other hand, there's a lot of tedious work. There are times when you're a prisoner of your own success, where you booked a bunch of projects, and then you have to deliver those projects. And there are only so many hours in the day. The older and more experienced I get, the harder it is to work with junior people. And I want to be clear about that: it's not that there's anything wrong with people who are young or inexperienced, it's that when you're the most experienced person in the room, but you really kind of report to people who are learning on the fly, it's hard. So, that's somewhat tedious, but the good outweighs the bad.

If you want to jump into being an analyst, make sure you're comfortable with writing and being a productive writer. You can be a good writer, but an unproductive writer. But you have to be both good *and* productive. I would also say work on your communication skills, and—really important—work on your analytic skills. There's a lot of common wisdom in the world, and common wisdom is wisdom, but it's common. And I think the successful analyst is the one who has uncommon wisdom. Ask yourself a lot of questions.

If there's common wisdom, why is it common wisdom? Or is there some alternative school of thought? What's the evidence that backs the common wisdom up? What's the outcome of that evidence? It's really looking at an issue across multiple angles versus just understanding the basics. That's another thing that separates the strong analyst from the pedestrian analyst—the ones who are thinking through issues from a much more astute angle.

I would say it's not a financially motivated career path. You can do fine, and you can do well if you reach a certain level of seniority, but you could easily take that experience and that level of seniority and make a lot more in the industry. So, it's a question of lifestyle, skill sets, motivations, and priorities.

So, the future's uncertain for the industry analyst business. If you look at the Gartner model, it is very tied to extreme segmentation of technology. In the little world of IT security, there is a firewall person, an IDS/IPS person, and a web gateway person, and so on. Then they put magic quadrants out for all of those. I think IT and security supporting it are changing so much that they're going to impact the analyst market.

Greg Young

> Greg Young first worked in Gartner's consulting organization. He came back to Gartner just as I was preparing to leave. He was at Gartner for 14 years.

I'd worked in IT security my whole career, in most every role from accreditation in the military, CISO, hands-on, encryption and firewall product companies, to consulting. I'd met a Forrester analyst at a conference early on in my career and thought it was one role I hadn't done and it would leverage the varied roles I'd had. In consulting, I had picked the company to work for by choosing the one with the best brand and people to learn from, so I chose Gartner. They weren't hiring analysts so I went in as a consultant. At that time, the structure of Gartner Consulting was not a fit for security, and there was almost no interaction with the analysts. But I took time away from billing to give my observations from the field to the research team. I left after a few years to run a very large security consulting practice and after about a year or so was called by Vic Wheatman, who was the head of Gartner Security at that time, and was told they wanted to bring me back as an analyst covering Network Security. I am guessing that collaborating and not embarrassing the brand with goofy findings were why I was asked. The core netsec team at that time was John Pescatore and this guy from Detroit named Richard Stiennon. I was an analyst for about 14 years of my 32 years in technology security.

What do you think makes a good industry analyst? What traits, habits, background?

Curiosity, collaboration, principles, intellectual honesty, and pragmatism are the traits. I don't think experience has as much bearing except that it really helps to have some foundation in an end user organization so that there isn't any detachment between analysis and reality of how the sausage is made. Curiosity is important because analysis must be based on the past, present, and future impacts and you have to listen more than you talk. There's nothing cringier than an opinion based on dated facts, or assumptions that are out of touch with reality. Collaboration is needed because almost all IT connects with and is impacted by other areas of technology or business. What better way to do analysis than to work with the analysts who work in those other domains? And more importantly, have a research position that is consistent. It was maddening to work for months to come up with a research position that was good advice to buyers and vendors, and then have some uncollaborative dingus make something up that is bad advice and start broadcasting it. Usually those tropes got more hearing because they were 'maverick' (i.e., imaginary), and those bad ideas didn't need a lot of research so there's more time for self-promotion. "Lazy is a special kind of stupid" was the memorable quote from one of our team. The best research came from an analyst who went through that Socratic stress test to refine ideas with collaborative peers. Those best analysts were the ones who took a lot of inquiries, then spotted trends that could be translated into advice that could withstand the poking and prodding of peers, clients, and vendors. Those stars also spent equal time around the spectrum between end users, vendors, and other sources. Being too weighted in the vendorscape alone can make you blind to the end user reality. The worst crimes are touting made up or artificial trends, being dismissive of new ideas, embracing every new idea without doing analysis, ever saying "time will tell," stating the obvious as radical or something that will occur only in decades, using the words holistic or synergy inappropriately, getting overly narrow in what inquiries you will take, and giving a new name or acronym to an already-identified area. Be OK with not being right in every discussion. Engage Socratically and respectfully, don't just be a loudmouth.

How do you identify a good research area?

It's not always good to pick an area that is 'hot.' That domain is likely already well covered, however it can be a good way to learn the business from a seasoned pro. Almost always best is an emerging area where questions and buzz are only starting and you can develop some basic ideas about how that market will develop. Then embrace it with the attitude that you have to become the world expert in that area, but conduct yourself like you never are.

Is it possible to pivot to other research areas?

Yes. In many ways you have to be constantly evolving with a coverage area anyway. Doing leaps to non-adjacent areas is possible provided you take the methods with you but do a RAM wipe on your brain for the specific content. The dynamics and physics of the new market are likely radically different and bringing in baggage is self-limiting and stifles curiosity. It also takes a reset in the level of confidence you operate with and recognize that "you know nothing, Jon Snow" and will have to play an exceptionally hard game of catch up to be able to provide valuable analysis again. Conduct yourself as if you've changed teams and have been sent to the minors for a while and no one there wants to hear about how you did things in the big league. I think if an analyst has been in one coverage area a long time it may not be possible to be as effective in that new role, but potentially would be more effective than a new hire. That isn't true for a closely adjacent market, or for unique individuals, as there are always exceptions.

Is the life of an industry analyst a good one?

It is mixed. To be a good analyst I believe you have to work incredibly hard, mostly by yourself. But with that effort can come defining moments of career satisfaction. Most days I'd be excited to see what inquiries and questions I'd be asked to answer. It surprises people that a Gartner analyst who works on the end user side of the business (giving advice to enterprises) spends the majority of their time on the phone answering client inquiries. Writing research was something that was 'squeezed in between calls.' It changed over time but it was common during a lot of my career to be on the phone more than five to six hours a day answering 10-12 inquiries from as many unique end user companies. Over time that reduced to about four hours with the burden of ever-increasing methodology and process. I learned so much every day. I always felt I learned more in a week of inquiries than a third-party survey researcher would learn in a year. With success comes challenge though, in that the more expertise in an area you developed, the more in demand you were for 'other stuff,' such as conferences and in-person advisory days that paradoxically left you less time to maintain that expertise. Burnout is the occupational hazard. Working closely with smart people and helping clients get answers were my drugs of choice. Truly smart people are usually very funny and great to be around. Many have become my best friends. Travel, bureaucracy, and politics were the down side. A group of experts can be either a championship team or a collection of conflicting superegos. There is usually an unreasonable amount of travel, and very long days. But coming out of the home office to get a coffee after helping a company solve a big problem that could change the trajectory of their business is very satisfying. The coffee was never as good after an exasperating hour of a vendor telling me the sky wasn't blue, if I hadn't answered a client's question to their satisfaction, or some troll under a bridge in the headquarters who had never written a Magic Quadrant was trying to tell me how to change them when I knew it would make it less meaningful to a client.

What was the high point of your analyst career? Low point?

The big high points for me were having a research position be recognized widely as valuable by clients. Those included a joint note with John Pescatore on *Defining the Next Generation Firewall* that was short but that we put a lot of work into, starting new Magic Quadrants that I was convinced were sustainable for at least 5 years, and a prediction on vulnerabilities that I knew was defendable and not just click-bait that is still reused today. I got to meet most of the CEOs and names of note in the industry and actually talk with them about the business. Career high points for me were being picked to be the lead analyst to cover all of Cisco's business (hundreds of analysts cover some slice of Cisco's offerings), and conference chair for the Dubai Security Summits. The low points were always the bureaucracy and the politics, never ever a client. Sure a vendor would complain to HQ that I said their baby was ugly, but I never took that very personally and knew they were usually blinded by love of their product, were not being strategic about what fight they picked, were being pressured by their management, or were right. The greatest low points were when the burden of the bureaucracy got in the way of giving clients the best advice, or when giving good advice to clients was devalued or wasn't perceived as being a valuable internal currency

What are some good tips for someone who wants to become an analyst?

You won't be respected because of the company you work for, you'll only be respected for the analysis you do and that takes time. You are your brand. That doesn't mean be a self-promoter, but let your research speak for itself. It is not all cocktail parties and conferences. I think I only went to a handful of conferences when I wasn't working at them full time in a one-on-one room or on stage. You need to be comfortable at a very high level with public speaking, writing, and working without supervision. Most analysts telework so that has to be something you are comfortable with. Know what you don't know. Get in some quality time with the family before you sign up. Be very honest with yourself about why you want to do it. If it is fame or money, you'll be disappointed.

Talk about the financial side of being an analyst. Is it a lucrative career compared to working in industry?

If you are doing it for the money, you're probably not employable outside that job and therefore shouldn't be doing it. If you're doing it as a springboard only to get a vendor job, your analysis will be suspect and you shouldn't be doing it. It isn't near Bay Area compensation but is closer to end user IT role compensation. The conflict of interest rules in most analyst firms mean that you can't invest in a lot of the tech companies. It's reasonable compensation for what for me was an incredibly intellectually stimulating career. I'd be a lot wealthier if I had done other roles, but the experience I had in the role was priceless.

Anton Chuvakin

Anton Chuvakin is one of the most prolific bloggers on his topic area: security. His career at Gartner culminated in the title of Research Vice President & Distinguished Analyst. He joined Google in June of 2019.

How did you become an industry analyst?

Somebody once told me, "Anton, you were an analyst for years before you actually joined an analyst firm," and this resonated with me. In real life, after one more vendor job back in 2009, I was doing some soul-searching while I consulted. All that soul-searching led me to start applying to a few analyst firms, however, avoiding the largest one... I assumed—mistakenly as it turned out—that the largest analyst firms would be more bureaucratic. As it happened, one of my industry colleagues worked for a smaller firm that I applied to. Later, their company was acquired by Gartner and that colleague reached out to me. Funny enough, I initially rejected his proposal because I was still nervous to join a very large organization. He convinced me that his smaller firm culture has largely survived and that I will like it. He was right and I did—and the rest is history.

What do you think makes a good industry analyst? What traits, habits, background?

I find this to be a combination of some expected character traits and career experiences with some more esoteric ones. From the expected side, the more critical ones are being able to work alone and remotely much of the time, plan and then execute your own projects and—of course—have a deep knowledge of the industry (cybersecurity in my case).

From the more esoteric side, you have to be BOTH "a talker and a doer"—you should be able to understand technology (as only a doer can) but also to be able to talk (and write) about it (as many doers do not, sadly—hence the need to be a talker). Another esoteric one is being able to learn largely by osmosis, via second-hand knowledge and interactions with current "doers"—implementers, practitioners, but also leaders. You will not have time to learn first-hand for many topics. It would be nice to have a lab, deploy systems, write code and such, but you are too busy.

How do you identify a good research area?

I look for a blend of exciting and real for clients. The trick—and it really IS tricky!—is to find the balance and ride the wave.

Here is an example: many clients called with patch management questions—in 2019. You may think that patch management is "so 1990s" and lacks any technology excitement, but clients still suffer from many challenges there and the need is real. On the other hand, pick strategic threat intelligence and threat attribution—this sounds like fun, but the client demand is largely not there. So, to me, a good topic is one with real interest from clients, perhaps a little extrapolating (i.e., slightly ahead of many clients, but not all), but also the one that has an intellectual challenge. Note that a good analyst would sometimes purposely break this and go to one side alone—this is how we ended up writing deception research, which we thought is very fun (while few clients asked for it) or research on how to use a vulnerability scanner well (which we weren't in love with, but clients clearly needed).

Is it possible to pivot to other research areas?

I've met very, very few people who are just good analysts no matter what they analyze, so perhaps their expertise sits in the area of "analysting" and not in any particular subject matter. Frankly, to be a good analyst you have to be a good subject matter expert in this area, and you do need to know more than most clients. That makes pivoting very hard, almost not worth it.

Is the life of an industry analyst a good one?
Yes, I would say so, definitely. As an example, I think I've practiced this pitch to new candidates for my former team. Here is what I usually liked to highlight: good work-life balance, very few (if any) work emergencies, only planned travel and interactions with really smart people—both clients and other analysts.

What was the high point of your analyst career? Low point?
This is a bit difficult, as this career has no obvious high point, unless you go into management, but then it becomes like any other career.

Personally, I made it to VP - Distinguished Analyst at Gartner and this is kind of their last step of the ladder. My only possible step up was to become a Fellow, but this is not really a rank, more like an honor that gives you some additional superpowers. I feel like people who stay and enjoy it basically stay because they enjoy it, not because they want to climb the ladder.

What are some good tips for someone who wants to become an analyst?
I think the key thing to develop here is a combination of "talker" and "doer" profile—in one person. This will make you a good analyst, and also a good CTO or a good VP of Strategy, so your effort is not wasted even if you don't become an analyst. You must combine the spoken and written communication skills with deep technical knowledge, otherwise it just won't work.

There is another trick to it that I mention here, too: When you guide clients you will need a particular attitude that I call "firm but not pushy" sometimes. In this business, definitely the client is NOT always right; moreover, clients come to analysts to get advice and to have their problem solved, not to "be right" (well, in most cases).

Talk about the financial side of being an analyst. Is it a lucrative career compared to working in industry?
No, sorry. Analysts are underpaid, and from what I hear they are underpaid at most if not all firms. What does it mean, though? To analyze this a bit further, a skill set and experience that you must have to be a good analyst will always earn you more at a vendor. Essentially, you sacrifice pay for work-life balance, stability, and a community of very smart people inside the firm. At one point when hiring, I basically openly said this in my hiring blog. So, this is a trade-off that you must want to make, otherwise, it not a happy story—or at least, not a long one.

Mark Bouchard

Mark Bouchard was an analyst at META Group for nine years. When META was acquired by Gartner, he opted to go out on his own. Through hard work and consistency he has grown the AimPoint Group into a valuable source of high impact content for the cybersecurity industry.

My Origin Story

Being stationed at NAVSEA 08 in Crystal City, Virginia, in the early '90s afforded me the opportunity to play a lot of volleyball on the Delaware beaches. Turns out, one of my regular opponents was a VP and head of the Global Networking Strategies (GNS) team at META Group. I guess he thought my engineering background was worth something—or maybe he was just tired of facing me on the other side of the net—because one day he asked me to interview.

That was in May of 1996 and several things stood out from that interview: it took place on a Saturday morning; it was with the entire GNS team (except for one Denmark-based analyst); and, at the ripe old age of 27, I was the oldest person in the room. Not only that, I was also the least technologically-literate person in the room. In fact, toward the end of the session, I told the team I probably couldn't even operate the phone on the conference table—it had 20+ more buttons than the 12-button phones typical of a government office at the time—but, if they wanted me to, that I would build them a submarine in the parking lot. I started two weeks later!

What mattered the most back then still matters today: confidence, technical aptitude, and the willingness to work 70+ hours per week, because that's what it takes to truly stay on top of even the narrowest of research areas.

A Recipe for Success?

I can't say I thought much about it at the time. In hindsight, though, this is what I believe it takes to be a successful industry analyst—and what I'd like to think I actually did for nine years.

With enterprise clients: Listen, listen, and then listen some more. Be respectful, humble even. You are not the only one in the room who knows something. And always deliver value. If you can't answer a client's question in a way that provides value, then please don't spin a line of bullshit in an attempt to save face. Tell them you don't know, then go find the answer and get back to them with it. Period.

With vendor clients: Start with the previous section. But realize, too, that it's not sufficient to rapidly assess a technology provider and just stick them in a box with a familiar label. Take the time to figure out the deeper details of how their solution actually works, what makes it different from others in the market, and how well it aligns with the needs of all those enterprise clients you're *listening* to. (Hint: reach this point, and you should have plenty of valuable information to share with both your enterprise and vendor clients.)

With your firm: Be a critical reviewer of the work your teammates produce. The all-hands research meetings on Thursdays at META were great for fostering such behavior. Fail to defend your position on a recent event in the market and you were sure to feel the sting, aggressively delivered by none other than your fellow analysts.

And let's not forget that the product being delivered here is research advisory services. So, for heaven's sake, do some actual research! Merely pushing tasty nuggets of information back and forth between the vendor and enterprise communities doesn't cut it. That's what lazy analysts do. The best ones take the time to think beyond the present, to apply the knowledge they've gathered, and to deliver meaningful, well-thought out projections of how the technologies and markets they cover will evolve over the next two, five, or even ten years. Fail to step up in this regard—for example, do nothing more than state the obvious in a research note—and you'll soon have to peddle your "didactic bullshit" (as Dale Kutnick used to label it with his bright red felt tip) somewhere else.

Bob Hafner's thoughts

Bob Hafner spent 28 years as an industry analyst. At first he worked for a Canadian distributor of Gartner but quickly joined as an employee. I had the great fortune of learning the analyst business from Bob. He was my hiring manager into Gartner in 2000. His contribution here is the richest writing on the business of being an analyst that I have encountered.

Falling into the role of industry analyst

Becoming an industry analyst was not a career decision; it was something I fell into. I had worked at a large Canadian bank for 10 years, building their national network of 1000+ locations and their disaster recovery plans throughout 1980s. I had moved into management at the bank and one of the other managers (Dave Neil), who was my mentor, had moved to a consulting firm.

Analyst Contributions

In February 1990, Dave Neil invited me to join the consulting firm to do telecommunications and PC consulting. The consulting firm (the Transition Group) was also the independent distributor for Gartner Group (now just "Gartner"). Within a few months of joining the Transition Group, Gartner asks if we could start writing a Canadian version of their US telecommunications research. This was done with Dave Neil, myself, and we were led by one of the owners, Frank Koelsch. We were paid by the Transition Group, but reported directly to the Telecom Research team at Gartner in Stamford, Connecticut. In 1996, Gartner purchased the Transition Group and Dave Neil, Mark Fabbi (who we had added to the team), and I became Gartner employees. I worked there until June 2018 for a total of 28 years. I had a variety of research positions, research topics, and research management roles throughout my tenure. I loved them all.

So that is how I fell into the industry, but the reason I remained an industry analyst for 28 years was enjoyment of the job. Don't get me wrong, the job did pay well, but the thing I loved the most was the client conversations. You would get on the phone or face to face with a client and would discuss a problem, a technology, or a plan they were trying to build. You would go through the issues and then you would give them what you believed, based on your area of expertise, the best way forward. At the end of the conversation, many clients would say, "this has been the best 30 minutes of my career." It was simply that rewarding. You really helped the client. The thing the client didn't realize was you just had 40 conversations about the same issue and had seen all the variables and permutations, so after hearing their scenario you simply needed to understand the specific context of that client to choose the right scenario for them.

The joy and value of the job was clearly quantified when we reviewed contracts and pricing. I still remember reviewing a 5-year, $100+ million per year contract for telecommunications services. This was at the time when optical networks were just starting to be deployed and several start-ups were offering some great deals. The client was ready to sign, they were happy with the carrier and the pricing was lower than they were currently paying, and the individual was extremely busy with significant network growth and the implementation of new locations. They just thought they would pass it by us to see if we had any suggestions.

The thing with an industry analyst is that we are focused on a specific area of expertise so we see a lot of detail about that specific topic. In this case, the size of the network was so large the client was not really interested in looking at alternative carriers, as moving would have been a huge undertaking. They were able to show they were reducing costs and that made their management happy. But the client was reviewing a telecommunication contract for the first time in five years and it may not have been the same person five years ago. As an analyst, I was reviewing 2-5 contracts a week, even more during the heydays of telecom. Their existing contract was overpriced so the discount the carrier was offering was still overpriced, especially in the ultra-competitive marketplace at the time. Based on my recommendations, the client was able to save almost $10 million dollars per year, or almost $50 million over the length of the contract. A million here, a million there, starts to add up to real money. On top of this, I improved response times to outages and improved penalties for not meeting availability targets. I don't blame the carrier; their job is to get the most for their services. An industry analyst's job is to get clients the fairest price in the current marketplace. Realistically, there were not many contracts that large, but there were many in the 10s of millions of dollars. I never kept a tally of all the contracts I reviewed but it certainly was well over $10 billion, and you can always squeeze something out, so if you assume a low of 3%, I saved clients very, very conservatively $300 million over my career. That's truly rewarding and it certainly makes you feel good, but what would have been nice is if I could have worked on a percentage basis.

I have been retired for almost two years, and the thing I miss the most are the amazing conversations with the very smart people within the analyst community. There were also many amazing conversations with vendors and clients. The conversations about the good, the bad, and the ugly of new technology, of a marketing strategy, or a software solution. The conversations about how the technologies/solutions would be used, how they would not be used, how they would be sold, at what price they could be sold, would clients use it, would clients buy it, would the company be successful, would the product be successful, and a 100 other permutations of what this technology/solution would do in the marketplace.

What makes a good industry analyst?

The perfect industry analyst is actually three equal parts in one, each is as important as the other.

First, they must be an analyst. They need to have detailed expertise in a specific area or topic and be sufficiently logical to be able to analyze and see trends in that portion of the industry. They look into their segment and understand the issues the end users face, vendors face, the direction of technology, the trends in the industry and how their research fits into adjacent sectors and the overall industry. An analyst needs to be able to see through the marketing material and industry hype to understand the real opportunity for the industry. Remember this is only a third of what they are.

The next third: they need to be a writer. It is of no value to have amazing insight and not be able to clearly write it down to share with people. Telling one client at a time will never get your ideas out. I cannot stress the importance of writing. In fact, we used to have a saying "if you didn't write it, you didn't say it." In other words, new concepts and ideas are not attributed to you unless you write them down, somewhat like copyright. I have seen more than one analyst upset when they saw a research paper with a concept or insight they had been talking about for some time written by another analyst. Simply write it down when you think of it, and then you know it's yours.

For the final third, the analyst needs to be an entertainer. As an industry analyst you will need to make presentations to share your ideas and to entertain people. I have seen extremely smart people get on stage, share amazing information, and put people to sleep. We used to call that the professor syndrome. I have also seen "analysts" get on stage and say almost nothing new and get the highest score at the conference. It wasn't about what they said; it was how they said it. An industry analyst who has a deep knowledge and understanding of a specific topic is of little value if they can't write clearly in easy to read terms about that topic. They need to be able to get on stage and get excited as they eloquently share their enthusiasm about the topic.

I'm not going spend a lot of time on the writing and entertaining part of the analyst, there are lots of books and courses on those things. I'd just say on the writing, I was very fortunate that I worked at an analyst firm that had amazing editors. They were able to convert my techno-ese content into easy to read prose. As for the presenting and entertaining, I did take a college course on public speaking. The most important thing I learned in the course was "to listen to yourself as you present." This is actually harder than you think. If you actually do listen to yourself, you will hear all the subconscious mistakes that we all make, especially the "umms," "ahs," and the changes in the levels of passion and fervor for the topic. Often, as you get into a presentation, you will start rambling, especially if you have a lot of information you want to share on the topic. This is because you want to make sure everyone knows how smart you are, especially about your topic. Try to listen to every word you speak as you present, hear what the audience hears, not what you think you are saying. It is harder than you think; at least it was for me.

Honesty and Integrity

Honesty and integrity are the most important traits of a *good* industry analyst. There are a lot of other traits that a good industry analyst absolutely needs as well, but if they are not honest and lack integrity, they won't be a "good" industry analyst for long. People want to hear what a good industry analyst has to say, the analyst can make or break a marketplace, a product, or even a technology. But if the analyst has been unduly influenced or even "bought" by a vendor, it is not long before people start to realize the product is not what the analyst has said it is. This is the start of an analyst's decline. It is not long before people start to question his/her opinions, which devalues the analyst. The short-term gain always results in long-term pain. Someone once told me "integrity is what you do when no one is watching." In the case of an analyst it should be that integrity is "what you do or *write* when no one is watching." I always remembered that when I was sitting at my keyboard by myself writing research.

I'm not trying to be a morality evangelist but I can tell you that there was always talk about specific analysts that were "for sale." Once you have been labeled, the moniker is hard to get rid of—just don't start.

Ability and Willingness to Learn

There are not any university degrees designed specifically to become an industry analyst, at least not any that I'm aware of, but I believe education is an important part of becoming a good industry analyst. It helps you to build logic frameworks, business and market understanding, technology understanding, writing skills, and the many other areas of understanding. But there are many places to be educated. Experience is education that you get on the job as you work. It's a matter of what you do with that education or experience.

Education

While it is not essential to have a university degree, it certainly was easier to get through the door of an analyst firm with a master's or PhD. Often the degree had nothing to do with technology or the research space the person was applying for, but a degree did demonstrate that the applicant had the ability to learn.

Experience

Applicants with a degree normally still had 5-10 years of experience in a technology space. Demonstrated experience and industry success could compensate for the lack of a degree, but it generally meant 7-10 or more years' experience. I did see some programs where master's graduates with no

Analyst Contributions

technology experience were trained in an analyst firm for a specific research area. The lack of real-life experience was a challenge for many of them and only about 15% became recognized industry stars. Based on that, I'd strongly suggest getting some real-life experience before you attempt to enter the analyst ranks.

The experience of taking a project from inception to completion is the best education an analyst can have. It is equally valuable from either the vendor or end user side of the project. Building a new communications network, implementing a new generation of hardware or software, the experience of planning, designing, implementing, and finally operating the initiative does not exist in any manual or specification sheet.

A plan is always clean, with well-defined steps. Rarely does a plan get implemented exactly as planned because there are always unanticipated issues. There are literally an infinite number of things that could go wrong. These issues are learned experiences that the future analyst needs to remember so they can either avoid them or anticipate them in their analyst role. These successful experiences will show the ability to take the strategic planning to a tactical implementation, and demonstrate the thought process plus the willingness and courage to change as the need arises. The future analyst needs to build a portfolio of these experiences, with successful outcomes.

One of my most interesting learning experiences was when I was still working at a Canadian bank back in the 1980s. It had nothing to do with technology, but educated me immensely. We were installing a new data center in New York on Wall Street. I was in charge of the installation of the communications equipment from IBM. Part of the installation included EIA cables (thick cables with 25 pin connectors). In New York, the electrician's union was very powerful, so while these were not electrical cables, they insisted on pulling the cables under the raised floor, but because they were unfamiliar with the communications equipment, they would allow us to install and connect the cables they had pulled. The electricians pulled the cables and left them hanging in the communications cabinets and then informed us that we could NOT connect the cables. It was only after they had installed the cables that they let us know that the cables were manufactured in a non-union shop and therefore could not be connected. The only solution was for the unionized electricians to cut off each end of the cable and re-install a new connector, which they did. The local facilities manager, who had experience in dealing with these electricians, had anticipated overruns, but even with his experience he was surprised by these actions. Fortunately, the facility manager had plenty of money in the budget to cover the costs; it did however delay the final implementation.

Finding experiences where you least expect them is sometimes missed by analysts. The whole point of an analyst's job is to help vendors and clients through changes in their technology or products. A good analyst must embrace change, but it must be realistic change.

Lifelong Learning

Technology is always advancing and as an analyst, you must always be current and have a willingness to embrace change. How can you help an end user make the best decision if you are unaware of the latest trends and developments in the research area you cover? Or how can you help a vendor developing product without the latest knowledge in that space? How can you tell clients to implement change if you don't accept it? You can't. This is why you need to daily read press releases, news articles, have briefings with vendors about their latest products and areas of development, and review many other sources of information. This is why you have to speak daily to clients about the challenges and limitations of the current products they are using or the ones they are implementing.

An analyst needs to remain current in any research space. An analyst's job is not 9:00 a.m. to 5:00 p.m. A typical week should be 50 to 70 hours as a norm, not the exception. Additionally, a good analyst will also learn quickly that Einstein was right when he said, "The more I learn, the more I realize how much I don't know." A good analyst will find the crevasses of knowledge they haven't entered before and learn, so they can go deep with a client or vendor on topics they are just discovering. Just one caveat, go deep but don't go so deep into a technology that you miss the point of it; i.e., you don't see the forest for the trees.

Learned Intuition

I believe people have different definitions or understanding of "intuition," so I looked up the word in the dictionary.

Intuition (noun): the ability to understand something immediately, without the need for conscious reasoning.

A good analyst learns intuition over time through the gathering of information, experience in the industry, and a lot of common sense. For example, once you have seen many marketing plans, and then you see the results of those plans—either good or bad—it's not long before your "learned intuition" can tell if a new marketing plan is going to fail or succeed within the first few slides of the presentation or simply on hearing the product space. The hardest part for me was to not interrupt the presenter with your concerns or approval until they had completed. And it is important to let them complete because in a few cases they had all the pieces of a great marketing plan but put the pieces together in the wrong way or presented it poorly. I remember working with one vendor that presented an amazing list of features and functions, but I hadn't heard of any people needing these capabilities. It was not until the second to the last slide of over 30 that they provided a valuable function that someone would pay handsomely for but they hadn't realized it. What was a shame was that they had already started the marketing and advertising plan, not focused on the high value function. We reorganized the plan and advertising and the product took off. It was one of those cases where the technology guys who built all the features (and were proud of them) also built the marketing plan. The problem was that they had primarily built a solution looking for a problem.

A real good example of an "intuition" I had was with Wifi handsets. This was truly a solution looking for a problem. It was the early 2000s, IP telephony was ramping up, Wifi was rolling out, cellular and cellular handsets were exploding, and the digital cordless handsets (DECT) had been around for a while. Somewhere someone thought we need Wifi-only handsets so we can walk around anywhere Wifi exists in the office. These Wifi handsets were targeted at the general office population, they were not ruggedized, they were not as intelligent as a basic cellphone at the time, Wifi coverage in most building was still spotty, Wifi handoff was almost non-existent, and worst of all the Wifi handsets were very expensive, almost double the price of a top of the line cellphone. So I asked a question, "Why don't you just use a good cellphone that has Wifi?" At the time the cellphone manufacturers were ramping up plants with the anticipation of building millions of phones, where the vendors of the Wifi handsets were likely pricing based on selling thousands or tens of thousands—orders of magnitudes less. The vendor's answer to my question was "cellular service is expensive," which at the time it was. So my response was, "Don't put a sim in the phone, in other words don't use the cellular part of the phone, it will still be more functional than the Wifi-only handset and will cost half the price, plus you won't have the manufacturing and repair headaches associated with running this business." This technology remained very niche and still is for the few vendors still manufacturing these for very specialized applications.

Hard Work, Not Luck

No analyst is successful by making lucky guesses of which technology or solutions will be successful or which will fail. It is about hard work, detailed research, and analyzing problems and solutions.

I must admit occasionally I did feel lucky when I talked to the right vendor when they were in a sharing mood, asked the right question of the right person, had a water cooler conversation with the right person or any of 100 other moments of chance. But a good analyst recognizes those moments and capitalizes on them. Perhaps "luck" is not the right term, maybe "chance moments" is better, but like someone once said, "You make luck through hard work." I believe that is true, but I did feel "lucky" when I had that chance moment and someone gave me the last piece to the puzzle I was working on.

"Can Do" Attitude

In the world there are two kinds of people, "can do" and "can't do." Can't do people look at a problem and then focus on why something won't work or why there are going to be endless problems if you choose a specific alternative. Can do people look at the same problem and then work to find the right solution to the problem. Can't do people will pull from their existing knowledge base and offer the easiest alternative. Can do people will pull from their knowledge as well, but they will research alternatives, talk to analyst peers, and speak with other clients and vendors to find the best alternative.

When solutions for a problem evolve and become the new standard, "can't do" people will be slower to adopt them. I have seen "can do" and "can't do" analysts and while both can survive, the best analysts are "can do" people. A good analyst needs to have that positive attitude, the willingness to look at many alternatives to not only find one that works, but to find the best and/or most cost-effective alternative.

Collaboration

Water Cooler Conversations

In the old days, industry analysts used to go to a place called an "office," every day, and that is where we would work. Very few analysts today work in an office; it is now the exception as opposed to the rule. Most work from their homes, with the majority of their meetings or interactions occurring through audio or video conferences—technologies we told our clients to use showing that we can take our own advice. But something I used to love in the old days was the happenstance meetings that would occur in the hallway or kitchenette with another random analyst. This could be an analyst in the same coverage area as you, but it was better if they were not. After the usual pleasantries, the conversation would turn to something like, "What are you working on?" You would share some details of the research and the analysis would begin. If the analyst was in a similar coverage area, the conversation would get into details and specifics, and often into the minutia of the research. The back and forth debate would always improve the research. At minimum, it would help to clarify ideas or concepts, and often enough it would result in breakthroughs in the research that neither analyst had considered before.

I remember in the late '90s Mark Fabbi and myself came up with the adage "hate is stronger than love." We had bumped into each other and started talking about a recent partnership between three companies. At the time, standards and interfaces were still evolving. If you wanted products from different companies to work together you needed to depend on the companies to have interworking agreements. A good number of smaller companies had done this for a while and it started to create portfolios of products that would work together. Some of the big companies wanted to play and co-opetion started to emerge. This is where two large companies setup a partnership to cooperate in one market where each have products that need to work together, but they also have markets where both have products that compete against each other.

Mark and I start to discuss what we thought of the partnerships and how successful they would be. There were a lot of these partnerships going on at the time and several of them were starting to fall apart. So we started to plot all the partnerships we could think of. Mark covered more of the data center networking technology and I did more of the wide area and telephony products at the time. We discovered that independent of the market, a partnership would fail if companies made partnerships to co-operate, i.e., "love" with each other in one market and competed, i.e., "hate" in another market. It was clear that the hate that these companies had in the competing market overrode the partnership in cooperative market. The other reality was often the reason they were competing in a market was because it was a big market, so executives of these companies didn't like that they could be potentially helping a competitor.

For our clients, this was extremely important to understand if they were buying products from these two companies and expecting them to work together. Clients would like to know the products will continue to work together for the life of the product, much past the first software update. In this specific case, the three-way partnership ended in about a year.

Times have changed. The companies have become really big. Standards and competition law now force these companies to either adhere to or publish interworking standards. As a result, most of these partnerships are no longer required.

There are patterns and cycles to technologies, and these patterns and cycles can be common across different technologies. Also, one technology can significantly impact other technologies as they change. This is why having discussions with analysts not in your research area is so important. A really simple but extremely impactful example is computing and networking. These technologies are tightly intertwined, but there are many analysts that focus on them individually. If these analysts didn't talk to each other and recognize cycles and patterns across these spaces, the industry might have evolved differently. Computing evolved through mainframes, servers, PCs, parallel processing, mobile PC (cellphone), and soon quantum computing, and got faster, cheaper, and more ubiquitous. Networking evolved through analogue, digital, optical, and wireless, and also got faster, cheaper, and more ubiquitous. But these evolutions did not occur on the same time scales. When computing got cheaper with servers and networking was still relatively expensive, we determined it was better to put the computing closer to the user to reduce networking traffic. This was the beginning of cycles of moving computing from central to regional to local and then the cycle again back to central as the cost and capabilities of networks and computing evolved. There are thousands of examples of these consequences and impacts that are highlighted when you look across research areas. It is really simple, everything is connected and everything needs to work together. There no longer exist islands of computing.

Perhaps the best example of an organization recognizing the value of random water cooler meetings in the hallway was at the Perimeter Institute. Although this was not built for industry analysts, it did a great job of acknowledging the concept. The Institute was a physics think tank set up by Mike Lazaridis, who was Research In Motion's (now BlackBerry) co-CEO at the time. The think tank would invite physicists from all over the world to come together to work for a period of time. They each had offices, but the Institute realized that as a physicist walked around, he or she may run into another physicist, and the conversation would turn to, "What are you working on?" So what they did was cover many of the walls throughout the building with blackboards. In that way they could share concepts and equations right there and then, and capture any suggestions or insights another physicist might have had. I think they describe it best:

The 120,000-square-foot building comprises blackboard-lined think spaces, casual interaction areas, formal seminar rooms, and a welcoming bistro. With collaborative opportunities around every corner, Perimeter Institute's home is an important contributor to the research culture within.

Research Meetings

A regular meeting with multiple analysts is something that you need to do regularly, and you need to do two different kinds: meetings with analysts all in the same research area, and meetings with analysts across research areas. Independent of the audience, the research meeting should be carried out the same way. You need a moderator, a presenter, and an audience of analysts. The presenter is there to share a piece of research. The analyst audience is there to listen to the research, provide constructive feedback, and make sure the research is clear, concise, and easy to understand. The moderator has the most important job—to keep the peace! Often new research will improve but sometimes shatters existing concepts, and if the analyst that developed the existing concept is in the audience, they may not be ready for their "baby" to be thrown out yet. This can result in very heated conversations or worse. The moderator needs to parse the personal anger or fear from the real issues in the research and remain unbiased, fairly assessing the old and new concepts. The goal is to get the best version and most reasonable vision of what this research should look like, and remove the personalities and emotional objections from the research. For some analysts, letting go of a research concept they developed, which became prevalent in the marketplace, can be very painful and emotional. A good analyst needs to look at the logic and details of the new research and then be willing to kiss their "baby" goodbye.

All research should be presented in a research community of similar analysts to ensure the research is technically sound. For research topics that are very specific or technical, this may be sufficient to allow it to be published. Broader topics need to go to research meetings that have analysts who span many research areas. You need to ensure that the research fits into the broader technology and solutions space without unintentionally negatively impacting existing practices; of course, that is unless changing existing practices is the intent of the research. More importantly, you need to make sure that "people" who may not be experts in the research area can understand the research concept and its broader impact. Having research that is so detailed that only a few can understand it is effectively the same as getting it wrong.

Virtual Collaboration

Now that many analysts work at home, the likelihood of bumping into another analyst at the water cooler is pretty low. This means the water cooler conversations need to be scheduled or planned "random" meetings. Simple things like phoning or video chatting with other analysts in your organization is a good alternative, but it implies you have to initiate it and you choose the analyst you exchange ideas with. You have to be careful to not continuously pick "yes" analysts that merely agree with most things you say. While it can be satisfying to feel like you are always right, it is less likely that they will challenge your concepts. Choose people that will test you, like many of the clients or vendors will. You want to be ready to defend your research.

The Most Important Collaboration

The most important type of collaboration was given to us by Einstein. He suggested that researchers need to do "thought experiments," which is effectively "self-collaboration." You stop and think about new research, and I mean physically stop. Start by clearing your mind and then building a workspace in your mind. Put the research in the center of the workspace, and then go at it from above, below, front and back, left and right. Go at the research with "what if" variations of the concept, competing alternatives, and basically try and rip the research to pieces. This is not a one-time exercise. You need to do this over and over again. I remember doing these experiments in the shower, lying in bed just before going to sleep, or upon waking up, driving in the car, or watching TV. Sometimes eating dinner with my wife or kids, they would see me looking out into space and they would ask, "What are you thinking about?" It was often hard to explain. The only way to you can defend new research is if you rip it apart and confirm its logic, just like clients, vendors, and other analysts will. Because if you are not prepared when you present the research for the first time, even friends will find its weaknesses. Use these thought experiments to improve and tune the research and prepare you for the inevitable blow-back.

The sole proprietor industry analyst may have some industry friends they can bounce ideas off of but it is much harder for them to collaborate. For them, thought experiments are the primary source of collaboration and they should make a concerted effort to actually do that. It will improve the research.

Identifying a Good Research Area

I'm Here To Help!

The reason clients and vendors use an analyst is because they need some help and they are willing to pay for it. Change is constantly occurring and they need to know the best course of action. This may also be change that only occurs once in a decade and the organization does not have the time or expertise to become current, never mind an expert, in the area. The spectrum of change could be small or large. It could be large like the planning and implementation of a mission-critical company-wide business system, or as small as the upgrade of a single piece of equipment. In the case of a vendor, it could be entry into a new technology space or input to a version release for a small piece of equipment. Change could also be the result of end user, vendor push, industry regulation, or 100 other reasons, but in all cases change is occurring and they want the valued opinion of an analyst.

Research Area Equals Job

There are two main factors in identifying a good research area. The first factor is "change." This can be "tectonic change" where the entire landscape of the industry is changing. Research areas that did this in the past include PCs, client computing, mobile, cloud computing, and soon artificial intelligence. This can also be much smaller "maintenance change" that continues throughout the life of a technology. Research areas such as network improvements, PC operating system upgrades, applications maintenance, and version control can fall into this class. Research areas go through cycles, in other words; once the primary tectonic change has occurred, the technology moves into maintenance mode until the next tectonic change. For example, networks went from analogue to digital to optical to virtual. Between each of these major shifts there was a maintenance period where the focus was more on capacity, vendor, and cost than the type of technology. While most think they need to be part of the tectonic change, the reality is an analyst that stays in the maintenance research space long enough will be part of the next tectonic change from inception. Plus, as I described above, helping clients get the best price for a service can also be very rewarding. The other reality is that all organizations do not go through the tectonic change at the same time, so even analysts that are leading the charge on the next tectonic change are spending the majority of their time helping clients with maintenance issues from the previous tectonic change.

The second and more important factor is the individual analyst. The analyst needs to remember that this "good research area" is their job. With focus and hard work, almost any analyst can become an analyst in any research area. The more important issue is whether they enjoy the area because this could be their job for a very long time. Individuals will have preferences and biases that can be a result of their upbringing, education, personality, or work experience. As an analyst, you need to find the research that you enjoy. There are thousands of topics: hardware, software, networks, architectures, security, and the list goes on. Pick one.

There are also great analysts that are successful at moving from tectonic change to tectonic change in different research areas and great analysts that move from maintenance topic to maintenance topic. While the tectonic changes can have periods of excitement, the importance and cost of maintaining the technology through the life of the technology is far greater than the implementation. Any analyst can, with time, do any of these, but the great analyst has a natural passion and understanding for the topic that fulfills their preferences and biases. That is why a great analyst will recognize the ease with which a topic flows from them and enjoyment it brings.

Plan Design Implement Operate

Organizations use the PDIO model when they implement new solutions within their organizations. The phases of a PDIO model are build a Plan, then Design a solution, next Implement, and finally Operate that solution. Each of these are phases of change that can be improved with the help of industry analysts every step along the way. I have seen analysts that take a single technology/solution through the full life cycle of plan, design, implement, and operate. Others have focused on a single phase of the cycle and have helped clients with the next new technology/solution coming into that phase or the maintenance of that phase. As an analyst, you need to become an expert in one or more of the phases of a solution that is being implemented throughout the industry. Fortunately, multiple technology shifts are occurring constantly so there is always opportunity. The analyst just needs to look and then choose the one that fits them and their skills the best.

Emerging Technologies

As new technologies emerge and organizations look to assume the technology, there is a clear opportunity for an industry analyst. Initially the analyst's work will focus on assessing whether the technology will be successful, what role it will play in the industry, who will use it, and most importantly, when will the technology be ready for enterprises. Once it is determined that this is a technology that will be used, the next role for the analyst is education of companies—how the technology works, whether it is technology that makes sense for them, and the speed they should be assessing the technology. Once we get to this point, organizations will begin the PDIO process to bring the technology into the organization, and here is where there is an opportunity and need for industry analysts throughout. Some great examples of technologies that have "emerged" in this space include cloud computing, software-defined networks, unified communications, and many others. Some examples still emerging include Artificial Intelligence (AI), edge computing, 5G mobile, quantum computing, Augmented Reality (AR), and blockchain.

Merging Technologies

Merging technologies is when two or more technologies come together to create a new solution or new technology. It could be argued that when technologies come together, they actually create a new technology that could be viewed as a new "emerging" technology. An example of this is networking and computing coming together to create computing where a single piece of equipment performs a networking and computing function simultaneously. Another example is 3D imaging and printing coming together to create 3D printing, and there are many more.

Another place where new technology is merging is with technology and non-technology spaces. For example, early work is occurring in human augmentation with biochips that connect humans with computing. There was another great example that happened years ago. A vendor came out with a product that did data compression. The product would recognize patterns in long strings of 0s and 1s, i.e., data. The founder of the company had worked on DNA sequencing in the health care industry. He had written an algorithm that recognized patterns in the sequence of amino acids in DNA. If you remember your biology, there are four amino acids, Adenine, Cytosine, Guanine and Thymine, but Adenine always pairs with Thymine, and Cytosine always pairs with Guanine. The result is only two combinations, just like in a data bit stream of 1s and 0s across a network. What they found was that the algorithm that was effective at finding long patterns in DNA (genomes) was also very effective at recognizing long patterns of data in data streams. Once they were able to find a long pattern, they could use a much shorter label to replace the long pattern and significantly reduce the amount of data that had to be transmitted. This was a vast improvement over what was currently available. I believe the improvement was between 50-90% reduction in the amount of data transmitted. At the time, data was growing quickly and long-haul communications links were still relatively expensive; the product paid for itself in usually a few months.

Another great place to look for research areas are in the gaps between technology spaces. In this case, the technology may not be completely merging but there may be connection between them and an analyst that can discuss how they connect becomes very valuable. A great example of this is mobile and applications coming together. An analyst that understands how applications are created and customized and also understands the limitations of the mobile device (i.e., the mobile computing platform) is still very valuable, not only from a technology but also a user-experience perspective.

I also met doctors who became analysts. They brought the knowledge and needs of being a medical doctor to the technology domain so they could recognize the products that truly addressed a doctor's needs.

The Best Research Area

It's not a matter of which area is the best research area, but rather which is the best research area for you specifically. The analyst that is self-aware of their strongest skills can find the research area that best fits them.

A Good Life

The life of the analyst is great one. Day to day you help people make important decisions, you help set the direction of the industry, and you speak with many interesting and smart people while making a good salary. I loved the job.

The best part of the job was conversations with clients. It was very rewarding to help someone with a problem or a question. Few clients realized that they were an important part of the research process. They represented data points that the analyst could use to track trends. For example, at the end of the month an analyst may have X number of similar calls complaining about problems with a product or a significant number of client's questions had shifted from "what is this technology?" to "how do I implement this technology?" These conversations all point to changes in the industry, trends the analyst can use for their research. The challenge was not with the content of the calls but sometimes just the sheer volume.

I loved to collaborate with other analysts; there were many amazing conversations where we built visions of the technological future. Some came to fruition; some were merely enjoyable thought experiments. There was never a downside to collaboration.

I loved to write, especially on topics where I felt I was slightly ahead of the rest of the industry, but I didn't always appreciate the deadlines.

I loved conferences. This was an opportunity to meet with end users face to face and get real life feedback on your research.

I loved the travel, even going through customs and waiting in lines at airports. You begin to build routines, and the time on route becomes part of your work day. Waiting for the flight was a perfect time to do email or just sit and go through a thought experiment, on the plane was the time to write or review research without interruptions. The one thing I do regret was not making more time to see all the beautiful cities I was actually in. In many of these cities I only saw the airport, a taxi, and a hotel. Vendor events were generally better at providing time and the means to enjoy the location. The problem with travel was that it generally was evenings or weekends, time I could have spent with my family.

I loved the recognition the job offered. Everyone likes to see their name in lights, getting quoted in prominent papers, interviewed on TV, vendors and clients coming to you for your opinion. It does feel good. I really tried to remain humble and level-headed but still enjoyed it.

No job is perfect, they all have components that you love and other that you hate. When I look back there were many more "love" components then "hate" components. It was always about the balance of all the tasks on my plate. There was never a time when I was not very busy and there is a simple reason for this. There are a set of tasks an analyst needs to do to perform their job and most are quantifiable, except for one. Tasks like write X pieces of research per month, talk to X number of clients per month, create X presentations per quarter, present at X conferences per quarter, complete administrative work on a daily basis, etc., were all easily quantifiable. The one task that was not quantifiable was to "become an expert in a technology space." There is not a metric that says "after X briefings, X meetings with vendors, X conversations with end user clients, and X press releases reviewed, you are now an expert in this technology space." There is always more to learn, there are always more new products, there is always change occurring, and constant change is why the analyst who is always current is so valuable. Clients expect you to be aware of the latest products, the latest innovations, and the latest failures. As a person that loves to learn and loves technology, the constant change was an enjoyable but time-consuming challenge.

All my experience was at a single analyst firm. I joined the firm when it was relatively small and grew with the firm. When I came to the firm, process was at a minimum. As a company grows, process becomes a necessary part of day to day life in order to ensure consistency of people and product. I accepted the process and the change that occurred, because I recognized that this was part of the growth of a company and the reason we existed was to assist in change. I know other analysts fought the process change.

In summary, the positives far outweighed the negatives, but there were negatives.

Highs and Lows

There are many more highlights, but the highlight of highlights was a set of research that Bern Elliot, Steve Blood, and I put together in the early 2000s. The three of us worked on this research as a tiger team for several months. We had weekly meetings where we discussed the issues. From every meeting we would have actions items that we needed to research or contemplate and then present the following week to each other. Along the way, we presented to several other peers just to make sure we hadn't strayed. The industry event that started this research was Voice over IP telephony (VoIP). For years voice and data networks were separate. Voice and data had evolved similarly from analogue to digital but had remained separate networks that used different protocols. With the introduction of VoIP they could now run on a single network, so we asked "where could it go from there?" Our research came up with the concept we called "communications enabled business processes (CEBP)." With any significant shift in an industry, you need multiple technology changes to occur in parallel. The tiger team found that in the business application space ERP (enterprise resource planning), vendors like SAP were attempting to automate business processes. The concept was to automate the process from when an order arrives, goes through the manufacturing, inventory, and then delivery with a minimum of human intervention. The process would stop whenever a human needed to get involved. With the arrival of VoIP it occurred to us that communications could now be integrated into the business process and the business process could directly communicate with the human that needed to address whatever the process needed. This could significantly reduce the human latency in the business process.

This research was well ahead of the market. Vendors and clients came to us to understand the concept and opportunity. Over the next few years this became a multi-billion dollar marketplace. The concept eventually became sufficiently ubiquitous that it is no longer a separate market. In fact, today all of us accept that while we are working in an application, we can click to move seamlessly to voice communications (CEBP).

There were some honorable mention highlights as well. Some of these honorable mention highlights were memorable because they were firsts in my career. The first time I was interviewed by the press for an article, the first time I was interviewed on TV on the business network, the first time I presented at a vendor event to other analysts, and the first time I presented to the board of directors of a multi-billion dollar company were all highlights. But over my career, I did these many times and they became less shiny.

Other unique highlights include the time they televised my presentation on stage with a live audience from the Grand Ole Opry in Nashville. I was proud when I sold and led an $800,000 consulting contract to help a vendor build a new market vision.

Another fun highlight included going to a Michelin star restaurant in Barcelona; it was delicious but we had arrived at 8:00 p.m. and when it got to 1:00 a.m. of the next morning and we were only on the eighth course of a 10-course meal, we had to tell them to speed it up as two of us had to present at 8:00 a.m. the next morning.

But the highlight of highlights was being part of a team that defined a multi-billion dollar marketplace months or years ahead of the rest of the world. We also received a thought leadership award, which was the cherry on top.

The low point of my career was when I retired. I missed the analyst life. I missed the clients, I missed the vendors, I missed the other analysts, I missed the travel, but most of all I missed the conversations and debates around the latest in technology with everyone in the industry. While this was a low point of my analyst career, it was the start of my new career. I retired to spend more time with my family, especially my grandkids, and that has worked out just fine!

Tips for Analysts

The Pen Is Mightier than the Sword

As you move up the ranks as an industry analyst you will start to get more attention from the vendors, end users, the press, and the overall industry in general. With greater visibility comes greater scrutiny of the research you write. Choose your words carefully, they can have unintended consequences. A poorly worded discussion of some minor problems a product is suffering could be misread as "the product is a disaster." A poorly worded discussion of a market that is slow to evolve could be misread as "this market will never happen." You need to be bold in your research but you also need to clear. Your words have power, so use them wisely.

Each Coin Has Two Sides

As an industry analyst you get asked for input in many decisions for end users or vendors. In most cases you get all the information associated with the decision, but there are cases where some information is omitted intentionally. It these cases you need to dig deeper to see the other side of the coin.

Why would end users not share all the information associated with a decision? One of the most common reasons is because the decision has already been made. In this case, the end user client would build a scenario where the only solution was the one they had already chosen, but they were looking for analyst confirmation they had made the correct choice. These were often public and government entities, who wanted to move the responsibility of the decision from them to the analyst. Then, when asked by a vendor that lost the bid, they could say the analyst chose the vendor without detailing the scenario they built in the conversation with the analyst. One of the most honest examples of this was once with a very, very large organization. The person in charge of the request for proposal (RFP) asked me to help him build the RFP so that a specific vendor would win because his executive had already committed to the vendor and they needed a public review of the winner.

In the vendor space, there are many reasons why they may not share information. It could be because they are buying another company, they are selling part of the company, product development is late, or hundreds of other reasons. You need to work with the information you have, but also remember there may be more that they can't share and that sometimes an "experienced" guess is required. A good example was with a vendor who had a product portfolio. There was a good product at the high end and good product at the low end. After the first few months it became clear that they needed a mid-end product, and I told them of this need. Initially they addressed the problem with installation of two low-end devices or occasionally a de-configured high-end device. This was not operationally efficient, so I suggested that they at least announce a mid-end product. After the better part of a year, they finally announced the mid-end product with an extremely short delivery date. I later discovered that they had taken my recommendation and began building a mid-end product immediately but did not announce it because they had significant inventory of the low-end product and knew once they announced the mid-end product, sales of the low-end product would dwindle.

Writing Skills

Skills improvement should be lifelong process as well. A good analyst builds, focuses, and leads with their strengths, but will spend time on diminishing their weaknesses. In many analysts, writing is a weakness. There is always a challenge in sharing very technical concepts in easy to read and enjoyable prose, so the reader doesn't nap halfway through.

Remember that when you make a prediction, these are opinions and not facts. This means that there could be multiple "opinions" varying the outcome and degree of a prediction. Very rarely is a prediction black or white, it tends to be varying shades of grey. But as an analyst you must have the conviction and build the evidence to demonstrate why your opinion (prediction) will occur. This means avoiding weasel words such as *may*, *might*, and *likely to occur* and using a definitive term such as "I believe this will occur."

Read and Listen Carefully

The goal of a vendor is to influence an analyst that they have the best, most successful product in the industry. This is marketing 101. As an analyst you need to parse through the adjectives and specifications in the vendor's marketing material to determine the reality of the product. It's the vendor's job to convince you how wonderful their technology is, how widespread it will be, and how quickly it will grow. Always remember (not sure who said this but it's true), "New technologies will have less impact in the short term than you expect and a greater impact in long term than you expect." So be careful about getting too excited about any new technology without a good fact base. The other fallout from too much excitement in research space is the desire to talk about this "wonderful" new technology. The more an analyst talks, the less they listen. An analyst has two ears and one mouth. A good analyst listens more than they speak.

Getting too far ahead of the next wave can be as bad as not seeing it. You only have people's attention for so long. If at the beginning of the year you announce, "This is the year of the widget," and nothing happens, then at the end of the year you have to explain why that wasn't the year of the widget, but next year will be. And if it doesn't happen again, few will remain interested and will likely miss or be disappointed when it finally occurs.

"I Don't Know" Is a Reasonable Answer

There is a perceived expectation that as an analyst you will have the answer to any question in your research space. This is unrealistic; there will be questions to which you will not know the answer. There is no shame in saying, "I do not know," and then adding, "But I will find the answer." This is far better than guessing or making up an answer. Spend the time and effort to find the person or research that addresses the question. Then, and this is important, go back to the client.

Original Thought

I personally didn't read research from other analyst firms. I read press releases, industry news, and newspapers, but not research from competing firms. I wanted to come to conclusions on my own. I know many times I did reach the same conclusions as other analysts, sometimes it was obvious, but other times I did not. Usually, I found out about those times I did not agree with other analysts from vendors who were getting research from every industry analyst.

I felt good about these times, especially when the vendors commented that I was more insightful. There were times when the vendors thought I got it wrong, but because I had come to a conclusion myself, I was always able to explain my logic.

You Are in Charge of Yourself

Success can change people. An analyst that builds strong product or technology visions and makes several excellent market predictions will start to get respect and notoriety. They will get called for a quote in the press or an interview on the business TV networks. There will be a level of fame, at least industry fame. It is what the analyst does with this fame that is important. Some analysts let their egos take control, they start to assume they are better than others, they start to belittle other analysts' opinions, and they often do this in an arrogant manner. A portion of these ego-controlled analysts can remain successful, but fewer and fewer other analysts will want to work with them. This is much like the stories that you hear in the acting industry: the actor may be exceptional, but fewer and fewer other actors and directors want to work with them.

There is a very thin line between being confident and being an asshole, and make sure you don't cross it. There is no reason, even as a superstar analyst, that you can't respect the insights of other analysts, and if you don't agree with them, you can logically debate the merits of their research without making it personal. Comments like, "Have you been living in a barn, that is 20-year-old thinking!" or worse, "Are you an idiot or just dumb?" are not needed to make a point. It shows how poorly an analyst has let their ego take control of them. A friend coined the term "confident humility," which nicely defines how an analyst needs to act.

One of my favorite analysts, who I considered a superstar analyst, was very humble and very precise. He would rarely interrupt and would also listen intently. I loved to work with this person. He was easy to debate with and his knowledge was far deeper than most imagined. During vendor briefings, he would listen to an entire presentation and then he would say, "Have you thought about..." and everyone in the room or on the call would fall off their chairs as they were literally blown away by his insights. He would take criticism, reflect, and then either agree and thank the person, or politely present a counter argument with details and logic. Even when you didn't agree with him, it was pleasure to work with him.

Realistically, every analyst will have their own personality, but it's how you let success change your personality that you need to recognize and choose the kind of analyst and person you want to be. Don't be the analyst that doesn't know they crossed the line.

Which Hat Are You Wearing?

We wear many hats as analysts and I would argue that you actually wear a slightly different hat for every conversation you have. You need to understand who you are talking to, which implies listening before you speak. A client conversation generally fell into several larger buckets: 60-70% of the time it was an end user conversation, 25-30% of the time it was a vendor conversation, and remainder of the time was either press or financial analysts. Occasionally, you would speak to other analyst firms at events or briefings which required you to wear a different hat again. There are several key questions you need to ask to build context for the conversation before you start to talk.

Name?

Getting the person's name and using it makes the conversation more personal, which means the person is more likely to trust you. This was one of my biggest challenges as I'm more of visual person. I would always recognize faces but would often forget names shortly after the conversation. It required several meetings for me. An analyst will meet thousands of people, especially at a conference, and should make an effort to learn names and remember them. Additionally, this is just polite!

Company and Title?

The company and title will tell you if the person is end user, a vendor, the press, a financial analyst, or another industry analyst. Be careful, you need to use both pieces of information to figure out where they fit into the industry. For example, they may work for a company that is a vendor, or has press people, financial analysts, or industry analysts, but they work in the IT department, which makes them an end user. You then need to parse their title further. If they are an end user, are they part of the planning, design, implementation, or operations team? If they are a vendor, are they part of marketing, product development, or sales? If they are the press, financial, or industry analyst, they will want to have a conversation about your research.

Current Environment and Issue?

The current environment provides the background of what is already in place in their organization, which allows you compare them to others in the industry.

Finally, the issue is what they really wanted to have the conversation about. Throughout this information gathering process, don't be afraid to ask clarifying questions because it not uncommon for important information to be left out because the person is embarrassed about previous decisions, especially as they look back in retrospective.

The conversation can now begin.

The End User Hat

The conversation with an end user client usually required the most detail to get the proper background and context. The title of the person will usually tell you where they fit into the IT space, and if not, ask them. The analyst should now have identified the technology space and role the end user plays as either part of the planning, design, implementation, or operation of the systems. Next, as part of the current environment discussion, the analyst needs to determine the company type. Is the company a Type A company, who are early adopters of new technology and are willing to work with a vendor to finalize the development of the technology because of the competitive or financial value the technology will offer them? This normally represents 10-15% of the marketplace. Most likely they will fall into the largest category, a Type B company. This represents 70-80% of the market. These are companies that use new technologies once the initial bugs have been worked out and the products have become relatively stable. The remainder of the market are Type C companies. They are slow to adopt a new technology and often wait until the next generation of technology is starting to be adopted before they adopt the current generation of technology, i.e., they are always a full generation of technology behind the majority of the marketplace. What is interesting is that these classifications are on a technology-by-technology basis and is not companywide. So, a company could be a Type A in one technology space, Type C in another, and Type B in many others. Once this background and context is understood, you then can deal with their questions knowing which role they play in addressing the issue and where the company exists in the evolution of the technology under review.

The Vendor Hat

Conversations with vendors were unique as there were two distinct categories. One category was a paying client and second category was as a vendor with product in the marketplace. As a paying client, understanding if the person is from marketing, product development, or sales helps to frame the type of conversation. As a vendor client, they will use the analyst as an information source usually to gather three pieces of information in the context of their specific role within the vendor (be it marketing, product development, or sales). First, they will want to know what are we saying about the vendor and their products; second, what are we hearing "publicly" about other vendors and their products; and finally where do we think the market is going. They would use this information to address shortcomings in their products and plan for the next generation.

The second category of conversation is more focused on the vendor briefing. This is where the vendor shares information, as opposed to gathering it. An analyst needs to remain current, which means getting briefed by many vendors who may or may not be clients. Knowing the full spectrum of products and solutions available is important for analyst to be able to best address the needs of their end user clients. For the vendor, it is beneficial to brief the analyst, as they know the analyst will be having conversations with end users who could be potential customers of their products. But you want all vendors to be clients, so the key is to let them know that vendors who are clients will get valuable feedback on the briefing.

Independent of whether the vendor is a client or not and independent of the category of conversation, the analyst needs to remember that an important goal of any conversation a vendor has with an analyst is to influence the analyst. As an analyst, you need to look through the marketing hype, the specification mumbo-jumbo, and latest industry hype and determine the real value of the new product or technology. Be careful of the bandwagon that can follow "the next big thing" and the vendor pushing it. End user clients are counting on you to help them make the best decision regardless of all the industry hype and vendor fanfare.

The Press Hat

The reason a press person wants to have conversation is because they are writing an article or story and are looking for insight or an opinion from the analyst. The analyst is having the conversation for visibility from a quote in the article. On its face it may appear as a symbiotic relationship, but often the press person has been tasked to write a specific article. The press person may be looking for a specific opinion, which might not be the same as yours on the topic. Their goal is get opinions that reinforce points they are trying to highlight in the article. The analyst needs to be careful of what they say and say it with great clarity. It is quite possible that the press person will deconstruct questions into very detailed segments in the hope the analyst will say something that will agree, at least to a portion, with the topics in the article they are trying to write. A good analyst will recognize what the press person is trying to do, and actually work to help the press person to understand the analyst's view and perhaps get the press person to re-think the goal of their article, or at minimum put multiple opinions into the article.

The Financial Analyst Hat

A financial analyst's job is to assess a company and determine how they will do financially. An industry analyst can be very helpful to them, by sharing their opinion of the potential growth of a technology market or the product viability of a specific technology company. But the industry analyst has to be careful not to do the financial analyst's job. Things such as financial forecasts, stock predictions, and a variety of other financial assessments could have regulatory or legal implications, and unless the industry analyst is also registered and trained as a financial analyst, they need to be careful not to cross that line.

The Industry Analyst Hat

Conversations with other industry analysts should be straight forward. If the other analyst is part of your organization, the conversation should be a wide-open debate. If the conversation is with an analyst from another firm, there is a dance that occurs depending on the relationship you have with that analyst and how competitive it is in the analyst marketplace. I found in general that sharing general information and basic insights was very congenial, especially if the research had already been published. Often the other analyst firm had come to many of the same conclusions. The area where the dance can get interesting was when you had come to some market-changing conclusions and you felt you were well ahead of the rest of the industry.

Confidentiality

The industry analyst needs to recognize in every conversation what is confidential and what is not. There are many different scenarios. I have tried to identify the most common, but integrity and common sense should play a primary role in the decision of what to share or not. If you are unsure, err on the side of confidentiality.

When having a conversation with anyone, you can never share the name of another end user company dealing with the same issue, unless it is public or the company has given specific permission to do so. Using the aggregate of many companies without identifying individual companies is fine and is actually an excellent way to identify industry trends.

Conversations or briefings with vendors can have confidential components. For the analyst, this can be a problem because it now means you cannot discuss the product or explain why you may still be positive or negative about a company or product. This was why as an analyst, I resisted or minimized the amount of confidential information I received. And in every case, there was a very specific timeframe for how long the information remained confidential. The reason a vendor may share confidential product directions or releases was to demonstrate that they understood where the market was going and provide confidence to the analyst that the vendor will remain a long-term player. The responsibility here is for the vendor to very specifically identify what is confidential and the timeframe.

People Are People

A good analyst needs to be able to speak to anyone at any level in any organization. The analyst needs to have the empathy to understand the individual and the challenges they face. They need to recognize that the CIO wants a strategy discussion, the technician wants a technical conversation, and vendors want an industry conversation. The analyst needs to value the client's position and opinion, but not let it change the analyst's opinion. Through respectful debate they can share their opinion and recommendations.

CEOs, executives, and founders of some these technology companies have become rich, some even billionaires. Clearly along the way they have made some good decisions and developed good products. That does not mean they are never wrong and that you need to be in awe of them. Most have earned your respect, but they are not gods to be admired and not questioned.

So even when you are a multi-billionaire, you are still a normal person at the core and live by the same values as the rest, but with a bigger budget.

Money

I learned early on that there is ALWAYS someone making more money than me. I also learned there were significant numbers of people making less than me, as well.

When I look at the industry, I segment it into three cohorts of workers: the end users, the vendors, and the influencers. Within the influencers, I include industry analysts and consultants. I start with a caveat: within each cohort there are always exceptions, with individuals that are either significantly higher or lower than the general population of that cohort.

When we compare salaries of end users to influencers, I believe the influencer does financially better than all but the most senior management end users. This is especially true when you compare the technical end users to influencers. Even end user management is not likely to do as well as a good mid-level influencer.

It is a much tougher assessment when comparing vendor employees to influencers. This is one where years of experience, job description, and the actual company will be defining factors. I believe a mid-level vendor employee and a mid-level analyst are close based solely on salary. A big differentiator can be the company they work for. If the company is a startup, stock options or profit sharing can significantly influence total pay.

Within the influencer cohort I would say that the majority of time the mid-level analyst would do better than the mid-level consultant.

An interesting metric to view is where people move to and from. The assumption is that they are moving for advancement.

End User to Analyst

I often interviewed end users applying for an analyst position. There was some success here, but the end user experiences were not always optimally aligned with what makes a good analyst. End users tended to have a much broader scope of experience, which meant their depth in the specific topic we were looking for was weaker than required. I also found the writing skills of most end users lacking as well.

Analysts moving to the end user space was not common, and usually meant they were going to a senior position in a large company.

Vendor Employee to Analyst

Movement between the vendor and analyst community was by far the most common and occurred in both directions. I often saw mid- to low-level analysts moving to mid-level vendor positions, equally I saw mid- to low-level vendor employees moving to mid-level analyst positions. I also regularly saw mid- to high-level analysts moving to senior vendor positions; however, there was only the occasional mid- to high-level vendor employee that moved to a senior analyst position. Most of the high-level movement of vendor employees was between vendors, with stock and profit sharing being an important component of their compensation.

Analyst from Consultant

This was almost exclusively consultant to analyst. I cannot recall a successful analyst that became a consultant.

A Curmudgeon

Curmudgeon is a term often used to describe industry analysts. I don't think this a personality trait of analysts, but rather a perception that results because good analysts "understand." A good analyst understands the complexity required to take a new technology from inception through development, production, manufacturing, marketing, sales, deployment, implementation, operation, and support. Analysts have the same understanding of the complexity for software or some other solution. From this understanding we know that 100% of these products will never achieve the high goals that the vendor is initially promising, and a significant number will fail completely. This understanding is why we do not immediately jump on bandwagons, why we question vendors, their marketing, and their specifications, so we can better understand the technology/solution and the likelihood of its success. But by understanding this complexity, one is often perceived as someone who is bad-tempered or just mean—a curmudgeon.

So, when someone calls me a curmudgeon, I take it as a very positive compliment, because it means they believe I have demonstrated that I understand the complexity of the marketplace, i.e., I'm a good industry analyst. Thank you!

Parting Shot

My last thought has nothing to do with being an industry analyst, it is simply a smart business rule. When I was young and just starting out, my father said to me, "Good things happen to good people." It seems obvious and I have tried very hard to live by that adage throughout my entire career and personal life. As an industry analyst, it is much easier to be destructive in your comments or criticism. I believe you need to try to have the harder conversation where you are constructive. Politely point out the problems and help with the answers. Even when you are having a destructive conversation, there is always a nicer way to say things that keep the conversation going, helping move the project forward. This will reflect much better on you. I have heard analysts tell a vendor, "This product is crap and here are the problems." It is more likely the vendor will want to pay and work with you if you say the exact same thing positively— "I see some shortcomings in your product and here are a few I would work on immediately." You don't need to reduce the level of criticism; you just need to deliver it professionally.

I know I'm getting old and sentimental, but I was an industry analyst for 28 years and I like to think I was a good person. I hope others think so as well, but what I can say for sure was that good things did happen for me. So be good, it can't hurt.

Success

When I started writing this book eight years ago I worried about encouraging people to jump right into the analyst world. Most of the analysts I know, and all of those that have shared their stories within these pages, were hired into analyst firms. Was it advisable to encourage people to go independent even if they had never been an analyst?

As this book came together in a mad rush due to enforced quarantine in 2020, I realized that by sharing my own experience and that of the contributors transfers knowledge that could indeed be used by an industry expert to not only transition to the world of industry analysis but to be successful at it.

I look back on all of the guidance here and think that, while concise and direct, it may well serve to talk someone out of taking the plunge. That is fine. In 99% of all entrepreneurial endeavors, you will be better off financially if you don't do it. But it is difficult to talk an entrepreneur out of doing the thing that is burning inside them. If you have absorbed all the ins and outs of being an analyst, and thought about the risks, and imagined the day-to-day grind; if you have determined through introspection that you have the traits of an analyst—you like to write, and speak, and you love accumulating knowledge and having insights—then you are going to enjoy this journey. And you will most likely succeed.

So let's talk about success.

First, financial success. If this means being able to support yourself and your family, maintain and even pay off a mortgage, travel, indulge your outside interests, put your kids through college, and save for retirement, then setting yourself up as an independent analyst is a good way to go. I would even go so far to say that the risks are low. There will be bumps along the way. The biggest hurdle in my experience is learning to even out your cash flow so that you can pay estimated taxes on time. At the end of your most successful year ever, when you feel that finally things are going to turn out, you may discover that you are

Success

staring at a tax liability of $100,000. Don't fret. You have several months before the tax is due, and you are probably making money at the rate of $40k a month. Start paying down that tax liability. The tax authorities are not going to arrest you (assuming you report all of your income). When the deadline hits, pay what you can, and keep going. You will get very official letters and incur interest and penalties. Think of them as an expensive loan and pay them off first. Then keep paying the rest of the year to get ahead for once.

Remind yourself that income tax difficulties are a sure sign that you are doing something right. You are making money! It may not seem fair that you pay more in taxes each year than you used to make in total, but that is how it works.

Job satisfaction. Bob Hafner described the best part of being an industry analyst for him was when he provided advice that caused people to say, "This has been the best 30 minutes of my career." That is peak satisfaction! Make note of those moments. Collect the praise for your work when it happens. Look back on your years of writing and presenting. The numbers will be satisfying. Try to document the impact you have had on your industry. Which vendors, taking your advice, went on to be acquired or went public? Who acknowledged you in their success? When did your predictions pan out? When did they not materialize? Analyze those results, too.

Freedom to explore new ideas for your business. As you get your head above water you will begin to explore new opportunities for expanding your business and perhaps generate some control over your daily work life. Are there some activities you enjoy more than others? Is public speaking the most satisfying? Can you do more public speaking and fewer vendor briefings? Can you get away from writing white papers if those become drudgery for you? Perhaps you can explore outsourcing the drudgery. Find freelance writers who can ghost write your white papers. Or recruit junior researchers to monitor the news for you or compile research on a subsegment of your space. You can take on retained consulting gigs with private equity firms looking to invest in your segment. Or you can start publishing better informed stock analysis to counter the number crunchers who do not understand how the business actually works. Or you can respond to opportunities that arise. Be an advisor for a friend's startup, or even sit on their board. Maybe even transition to an investor in startups or public companies, keeping in mind that you have to avoid creating conflicts. You can explore transitioning to an online subscription model. Can you package all your research into something that people will pay to get access to?

You may even discover how to expand your firm by hiring and training analysts. Start to transfer your brand to them so that they too can start to earn good money. This book is light on advice on how to do that, probably because

I don't have personal experience doing it. But the founders of all the big firms did just that, and at least one of them, Patrick McGovern of IDG, became a billionaire. There will always be a demand for curated knowledge that helps decision makers. Turn your analyst's mind to the problem of what form will that curation take in the future? Can you recreate a PitchBook or Crunchbase model in your space? One that people are willing to pay for?

Along the way you may discover that writing is your passion. Your columns and books may be well received and even contribute to your financial success. Should you spend more time writing books to create that source of recurring revenue? Can you follow in John O'Reilly's footsteps and create a publishing house?

You can see that not only is there not one path to success as an industry analyst but that success leads to many more paths that you can take. One path may lead nowhere but another could open up more paths, each leading to accumulated successes. Follow as many paths as you have time and energy for, always staying true to the honesty and integrity that Bob Hafner stresses. Bring as many people as you can along with you. Who can claim that having options while doing what you love is not a successful life?

THE END

Appendix I Writing Resources

Speaking primarily about works of fiction, James Branch Cabell said the goal for an author is to write perfectly about beautiful happenings. That is a lofty goal for any writer, and perhaps over the top for nonfiction. Yet, why not strive to write perfectly? We may fail but are bound to have created something that is more enjoyable to read and conveys the knowledge we wish to impart.
Here are the books on writing that I have found the most useful and inspiring.

The Sense of Style: The Thinking Person's Guide to Writing in the 21st Century, by Steven Pinker, is my favorite book on style and writing.

On Writing Well: The Classic Guide to Writing Nonfiction, by William Zinsser, is a must-read. I have found it guided me in developing a voice for my research reports, blogs, and books. It was first published in 1976 and has been updated many times since.

Good Prose: The Art of Nonfiction, by Tracy Kidder and Richard Todd. You may remember Kidder for *The Soul of a New Machine*, one of the first narrative nonfiction books on the tech industry.

Writing Down the Bones: Freeing the Writer Within, by Natalie Goldberg, is a series of philosophical essays on writing that may provide some motivation.

Bird by Bird: Some Instructions on Writing and Life, by Anne Lamott, is another collection of essays to help you tackle and complete a project.

Creative Nonfiction: Researching and Crafting Stories of Real Life, by Philip Gerard, has chapters on conducting interviews, choosing a topic, and research which are a big help.

Steering the Craft: A Twenty-First-Century Guide to Sailing the Sea of Story, by science fiction author Ursula K. Le Guin, is beautifully written prose about writing beautifully.

If you find yourself fascinated by the writing life, as I am, you will enjoy Zinsser's memoir, *Writing Places: The Life Journey of a Writer and Teacher*.

C.S. Forester, one of my favorite fiction authors, also wrote a memoir: *Long Before Forty*. What is notable about Forester is that his writing appears effortless. The reader can be completely absorbed in the story without being distracted by the writing at all.

In the same vein as Forester, Nevil Shute's memoir, *Slide Rule*, describes how he transitioned from pioneering aeronautical engineer to bestselling author of such works as *A Town Like Alice* and *On The Beach*.

I encourage you to read these works and also look up your favorite authors on YouTube. Many of them have lectured on their writing practices. Malcolm Gladwell teaches a master class at masterclass.com which is revealing and practical.

Oh, and one more. Jon Winokur's *The Portable Curmudgeon*, a collection of over a thousand quips and quotes from notable curmudgeons, from Groucho Marks to Dorothy Parker.

Appendix II Analyst Firms

ARInsights has created the most popular tool for managing analyst relations. Think Salesforce for AR people. As of this writing, they report that they track 7,515 analysts working at 1,039 firms. As you enter the analyst business, especially if you are launching your own firm, make sure that you are included in their database.

Here is a list of the top 100 analyst firms ranked by the number of analysts they employ. Note that with 1,008 analysts, Gartner employs 13.4% of the analysts tracked. Keep in mind that while ARInsights tracks management consulting firms, they are not likely to track industry analysts embedded in other types of companies; the competitive analysis function, for instance.

You will notice that there is a rapid drop in number of analysts that make up a firm. Only the top five employ more than 100. The bottom four firms (in the top 100) only employ five analysts each. The other 939 firms not included here are small, yet I would predict doing very well for themselves. That, after all, is where IT-Harvest sits. Note that The Analyst Syndicate, formed by Tom Austin, has 24 analysts. I am a member of this group, which brings together independent analysts to leverage their breadth of industry coverage and pool resources for sales and marketing efforts.

Firm	Number of Analysts
Gartner Inc.	1008
IDC	766
Omdia	289
Forrester Research, Inc.	256
Frost & Sullivan	147
IHS Markit	86

Firm	Number of Analysts
451 Research	77
Everest Group	76
GlobalData	62
Strategy Analytics, Inc.	62
Analysys Mason	51
ARC Advisory Group	47
Aite Group LLC	41
ISG (Information Services Group)	36
ABI Research	33
GSMA	33
Celent LLC	29
Greenwich Associates	27
teknowlogy PAC	25
Info-Tech Research Group (ITRG)	24
Technology Business Research, Inc. (TBR)	24
The Analyst Syndicate	24
Enterprise Strategy Group (ESG)	23
Navigant Research	22
BCC Research	21
PhoCusWright, Inc.	20
Counterpoint Technology Market Research	19
KuppingerCole Analysts AG	19
GovWin by Deltek	18
S&P Global Market Intelligence	18
BARC (Business Application Research Center)	17
Canalys	17
Futuresource Consulting Ltd.	17
HFS Research	17
Ecosystm	15
NelsonHall	15
Keypoint Intelligence	13
Pharma Intelligence	13
TeleGeography Research	13

Appendix II Analyst Firms

Firm	Number of Analysts
eMarketer Inc.	12
G2	12
GigaOM	12
KLAS Enterprises LLC	12
Novarica	12
CONTEXT	11
Information Technology Research (ITR) Corporation	11
MarketsandMarkets (M&M)	11
Mintel International Group Ltd.	11
Moor Insights & Strategy	11
TechVision	11
CCS Insight	10
Enterprise Management Associates (EMA)	10
gap intelligence	10
Jane's	10
Javelin Strategy & Research	10
Outsell, Inc.	10
Arete Research	9
Bluefield Research	9
Heavy Reading	9
Market Intelligence and Consulting Institute (MIC)	9
NPD Group	9
Parks Associates	9
TechMarketView LLP	9
Twimbit	9
Wainhouse Research, LLC	9
Argus Research Company	8
Berg Insight AB	8
Chartis Research	8
Constellation Research, Inc.	8
Crisp Research	8
Dell'Oro Group	8
DigiTimes Research	8

Firm	Number of Analysts
Enders Analysis, Ltd.	8
Lecko	8
Mercator Advisory Group, Inc.	8
Spend Matters	8
VDC Research Group, Inc. (Venture Development Corporation)	8
Aberdeen Group	7
Ampere Analysis	7
Bloor Research	7
Evaluator Group, Inc.	7
Juniper Research Limited	7
ACG Research	6
Aragon Research, Inc.	6
Cutter Consortium	6
Futurum Research	6
IBRS (Intelligent Business Research Services Pty Ltd)	6
IDATE Digiworld	6
LNS Research	6
MZA Ltd.	6
Northern Sky Research, LLC (NSR)	6
Signify Research	6
Technology Evaluation Centers Inc. (TEC)	6
The Group of Analysts (TGOA)	6
Topology Research Institute (TRI)	6
Verdantix Limited	6
Chilmark Research	5
Directions on Microsoft	5
Infoholic Research LLP	5
Interact Analysis	5

Security Yearbook 2020
A History and Directory of the IT Security Industry

A walk down memory lane for security practitioners, an introduction to the entire industry for students, marketers, and investors.

"Stiennon's experience and contribution to this industry makes him the best person to tell its story and his voice is the best one to guide us into the future."

— Gil Shwed, CEO and founder of Check Point Software

Purchase at www.it-harvest.com/shop

Made in United States
North Haven, CT
21 February 2024